THE
boyfriend
TEST

THE
boyfriend
TEST

How to Evaluate HIS Potential BEFORE You Lose YOUR Heart

WENDY L. WALSH

THREE RIVERS PRESS • NEW YORK

Published by Three Rivers Press, New York, New York. Member of the Crown Publishing Group.

Random House, Inc. New York, Toronto, London, Sydney, Auckland
www.randomhouse.com

THREE RIVERS PRESS is a registered trademark and the Three Rivers Press colophon is a trademark of Random House, Inc.

Printed in the United States of America

Library of Congress Cataloging-in-Publication Data

Walsh, Wendy (Wendy-Lee)
       The boyfriend test : how to evaluate HIS potential before you lose YOUR heart /
    Wendy Walsh.—1st ed.
       1. Mate selection.   2. Man-woman relationships.   3. Dating (Social customs)
    4. Marriage compatibility tests.   I. Title.
    HQ801.W275   2001
    646.7'7—dc21   00–060733

ISBN 0-609-80584-3

10 9 8 7 6 5 4 3 2 1

First Edition

For my late parents,
Ellen and Bernard Walsh.
Mom, thanks for testing Dad
and giving him an "A."

acknowledg- ments

Thoughts become a book when strangers in publishing have the intuition to sense that an author's story should be shared. Thank you to my editor, Carrie Thornton, and my agent, Jan Miller, along with Joy Donsky and her other associates who were introduced to me through the printed word and took my cause as their own.

It is surprisingly difficult to find words to thank the only person who knows me both as a preverbal person and an ardent adult talker. Thank you to the empathetic and ethical psychologist who helped me understand and trust my own feelings, Dr. Zari Hedayat.

To David Mirkin. Thanks for briefly stepping into my life armed (and you *knew* you'd have to be armed) with compassion, consciousness, and twisted jokes.

At various crossroads in my life I have been a single woman, yet I was never alone. Each time I was surrounded by a girlfriend or three who, knowingly or not, became sounding boards who echoed back the bones of this book. My gratitude goes to Sylvia Ahi-Vosloo, Kathy Beckley, Karen Geoffrey, Carol Iacovelli, Maria Jones, Lora McLaughlin, Nanette Pattee Francini, Denise Robinson, and Debra Snell. And thanks to my newfound "Mom" friends Jodie Coady and Ilsa Glanzberg for your support and encouragement.

I also want to mention with love, my brothers, Andy Walsh and Chris Walsh, whose sibling rivalry—and revelry—helped shape my psyche.

To Virgil McDowell. For staying the course during our personal storms, and sharing the ecstasies and challenges of parenthood with me. Most of all, thanks for "hangin in there" while I figured out who I was.

Finally, I would be remiss if I did not acknowledge the many men whom I have had romantic collisions with. My boyfriends have been some of my best teachers and none will be forgotten.

contents

introduction

It was a Tuesday night. It was two A.M. And I was in the back room of a nightclub kissing Dennis Rodman. Actually, sucking on his bottom lip would be a more accurate description. The saga of how I got there is as exciting as it is painful, and this night was certainly the climax. As the most notorious bad boy to ever play in the NBA scribbled his phone number on a cocktail napkin, a small surge of bile in my upper abdomen informed me that I had finally hit rock bottom in the search for a mate. It was time to find a real boyfriend.

Not to malign Mr. Rodman, of course. He is the recipient of some rewarding genes and has taken his gift of physical prowess to the max—preferring to focus on short-term relationships, perhaps to better make his own mark in the evolution of our species, or to medicate himself. More power to him. But the bigger question is: What was I doing there?

I am smart. Or at least I thought I was. At the time, I was a successful news anchor in Los Angeles. I stood five feet ten inches, was a blond, blue-eyed, blazered icon of young female success. Yet time and time again I was dating losers! Some very yummy-looking and often wealthy losers, I might add, but they were men who couldn't participate in a healthy relationship if their 401(k)s depended on it. I was in a pickle. Nice guys turned me off. Bad boys made me nuts. And my girls' club had become my surrogate "significant other."

Not that I wasn't *trying* to have healthy relationships. I bought enough self-help and relationship books to merit stock options with my local bookstore. But no matter how much I read and how much I practiced all that stuff about open, honest communication, about kindness and empathy, I just couldn't get my men to cooperate.

The Rodman incident was an epiphany. Because of his much-publicized track record of multiple, brief relationships and volatile marriages, Mr. Rodman was clearly the wrong man for me. When I stood near him that night, the unequivocal feeling of dread in my gut told me my heart could be marching into a losing battle, once again, with a bad boy— only this time I couldn't find a way to rationalize it. It made me reflect on all the others whom I had made so many excuses for, and I knew at that moment that I was habitually selecting the *wrong* men. So I took this revelation and went hiking in Switzerland.

Deep Breaths in the Alps Don't Guarantee a Clear Head

The seed of this book sprouted in the Alps. I was lunching with two elegant French women on the patio of their country club. They were friends of my traveling companion, who was male, but as I was ten months into a year of celibacy (that you'll read more about later), I might as well have been traveling with a girlfriend. Nestled in a lush valley, our "girl talk" was protected by a set of snowcapped mountains that Heidi would have longed for.

My companion's two female friends were mother and daughter, the former, Elaine, a beautiful woman in her early fifties whose manner and attire screamed *Town & Country* magazine. Her twenty-something daughter, Michelle, was telling the story of her mother's most recent heartbreak.

The catalyst was a Swiss-Italian playboy, a middle-aged stockbroker who had swept Elaine up in a romantic whirlwind. Specifically, he made room for her on his Harley-Davidson and charged up a mountainside blasting some heart-wrenching Italian opera through a set of headphones. Once at the top, he laid out a picnic and read her a French poem that brought her to tears. For this she closed her business and left her family and friends to move to the city where he lived.

Our luncheon conversation took place two years after the romantic hijacking. In the aftermath, she was back home, alone, heartbroken, and hurt that her paramour had never itment to the blessed union he had rhapsodized

.. ne most about this story was that Elaine is a
. woman. She is educated and articulate and runs a successful company, yet she seems to have made the same
mistakes as me and many of my younger, inexperienced
girlfriends.

Coincidentally I had met Elaine's "scoundrel" at his office
just days before my lunch with Elaine, and I had no problem
reading his m.o. from miles away. As it turned out, I was
immune to his lecherous advances since he wasn't my physical type. After he sniffed my disinterested pheromones, I
watched him hit on every woman who entered his line of
sight. This Casanova flirted with so many women, I wondered
if sexual harassment was yet to be deemed a crime in
Europe.

If I could see his antics so clearly, why hadn't Elaine, this
bright woman? The answer: She had no standardized guidelines on how to choose a reliable man. Neither, for that matter, did I. Thus, the premise for this book was born.

My Search for Answers

A premise is only the beginning of a search. Hoping to find an intellectual answer to heartbreak,
I began to read deeper and richer material.
(Celibacy provides one with *a lot* of free time!) I
was spurred on by the deaths of my parents (is death ever
timely?). That psychological wake-up call sent me down more

library corridors, to New Age bookstores, and to frequent hits on Amazon.com.

I needed answers to life's most confounding questions: Where did my parents go? Where am I headed? Who or what am I, anyway? Do I have a soul at all, or am I just squishy bits of smart-ass biology decorated by Seventh Avenue? And equally important, I wanted to know if a soul existed in the many heartless men I had been encountering. I'd begun to seriously doubt it.

During my literary meanderings, I was also warned by peers about the dangers of books. One player type whispered into the phone one night that he thought I might be "bookish." He said it just the way a man might call a woman "frigid." Then he declared that this research would surely sentence me to become a "recluse." He uttered the word *recluse* in an under-the-breath way that men in my mother's generation probably used when labeling old maids.

Since this guy was still single at thirty-seven and convinced that the key to happiness was in the stock market, I ignored his advice and read on. I read biology and anthropology to probe what is left of a being after genetic programming is accounted for. (And by the way, I found there's far more to DNA than what we learned in the O.J. courtroom.) In psychology books I searched for answers about how much of what we are is simply sponged up from our culture or dragged along, like heavy Louis Vuitton suitcases, from our childhoods.

I found some very enlightening material in psychology texts. And I noticed that while searching for general guidelines for proper boyfriend behavior, I was becoming more clear about my own boundaries in personal relationships. *The Boyfriend Test,* simply put, is a book about boundaries.

I found one startling statistic: An estimated one-third of American women suffered some form of abuse—sexual, physical, or emotional—in childhood. That's one in three of us, girlfriends! As children, those women were confused about what was happening, but since our abusers were often family members or loved ones, we tricked our brains into believing such treatment was okay. That thought pattern was then carried into adulthood, and today we have the quaint expression "poor boundaries" to describe women who are consistently shit on and don't squawk. Not that we don't feel pain. It's just that somehow we think the pain is normal, or worse, that we deserve it. Well, it's not and we don't! *The Boyfriend Test* is, at the very least, a general set of guidelines for women who need to assert their needs and desires.

This book is for me, Elaine, and the millions of women like us who have trouble seeing the red flags on love's racetrack. Instead we proceed, full throttle, heart in hand, toward a fateful crash, and wonder why we hit the wall so hard.

Dream Girlfriends and Dream Boyfriends Exist

My first inclination after charging through many men and many heartbreaks was to become a complete pessimist. I was convinced that the perfect man didn't exist, and that in order for me to have any semblance of a normal relationship, I would have to lower my expectations—which I did for a while and became even more miserable.

Let's face it, we're all human. We all have lessons to learn. And Dream Girlfriends and Dream Boyfriends are really just humans beings who are looking at their problems with an adult eye and attempting to change. The journey of life is about growth. You shouldn't go looking for a perfectly unrealistic man. Nor should you beat yourself up if your own behavior isn't perfect.

I use the term "Dream" here not to imply something unreal but instead something comfortable. Like a dream itself, a Dream Boyfriend has an intangible set of qualities, ones that make him a thinking, feeling, aware person. Likewise for you. The point of this book isn't to disparage men (or women for that matter) but rather to help you select a mate who is ready for the wonderful and challenging give-and-take of romance.

Man Shopping 101

Have you ever heard the little jewel of wisdom that it's possible to learn everything you need to know about a boyfriend candidate on the first date, if only you knew what to look for? I don't think this applies to every man—sometimes you have to take the time to peel away a few layers before getting to the juice. But I do think there's more than a little value to the concept. I have learned that it's possible within about five dates to glean enough vital facts about a man's ability to inflict emotional chaos. And that five-date window is usually plenty of time to escape with your heart intact.

Think about it. Take a moment and remember one nightmare relationship from your past. Now focus on everything he said or did on those fateful first dates. Did he allow you to pick up the check? Did he twice mention his love for strappy shoes? How about the fact that he helps out his dear old mother by paying some of her bills?

Sure, at the time you dismissed the first-date Dutch treat as a sign of a liberal man who might be an equal partner rather than a control freak. Today you have full disclosure about his financial mess relating to an old drug problem and a new alimony check the court makes him write. But why did it take you half a year and six sizable MasterCard bills to get a clue?

Or that strappy-shoe man. You thought he was refreshingly fashion conscious, right? Five dates later you're in the sack with your supposed Dream Man. He takes one look at your bunions and pump-bumps and forgets your phone number. On your first date he was sending you what he thought was a clear message about his foot fetish.

And about that man with the kind heart who treats his mother like a queen? You thought it might be an omen that he treats all women like royalty. Of course, you now know that Mom not only gets his money but also all of his love—and there's none of either left for you.

I speak with the voice of the walking wounded. The three examples I have just cited all happened to me. I'm blessed that, rather than bitterness, my lessons brought wisdom—and a tilted sense of humor. As you're about to read, my dating history has given me plenty of material.

Don't Mother a Relationship, Manage It!

I admit that I share a condition with an awful lot of women that I call the "female nurturer syndrome." It's a trait that compels us to treat bad boyfriends with good bodies too kindly. The syndrome forces smart, level-headed women to respond to their girlfriends' disapproval with the mantra "Give him a chance. He'll change."

Ha! I am here to assure you that, in fact, he may have the ability to change, but no amount of nurturing or Victoria's Secret lingerie will affect the timing of his personal transformation. He's got to want to make the change himself. Ten notes sent on cute cards or a hundred step classes won't make him treat you any differently than he did on the first date. That's as good as it gets. So it better be great.

All Men Are Basically Good, But It's Not Your Job to Make That Apparent

I once asked a criminal attorney, who is also a mother, to explain to me how she defends pedophiles. (Her firm handled the infamous pop star case that was dismissed.) She shared with me her professional motto,

"All people are basically good." To which I replied, "Yeah, but some good people are also pedophiles."

Likewise, some good men are also bad boyfriends. What I mean is that we all have gaps in our psychological and spiritual growth. Men are not bad people. They are mostly great people who sometimes have a few *issues* just like we do. But it's not our job to make each man a "project" by trying to heal him.

It is an individual's responsibility to become conscious of his or her issues and do something about them. And we generally don't become conscious of our issues through someone else's reminders. Admit it, did you ever listen when your mother nagged you to clean up your room? Likewise, no amount of female probing or pestering, however gentle, will change a man in denial. You can bring that horse to water all day...

You may not have cleaned your room at your mother's behest, but these days when you have a hot date coming over, I'll bet those sheets are changed and all your girl crap is neatly stored out of sight, right? The motivation: fear that your man will reject you because you live like a pack rat, or worse, that he'll spread the news to the entire male population. Yes, a no-show by the testosterone team is our worst fear.

So why do you still show up when a guy exhibits bad boyfriend behavior? Maybe he needs an estrogen no-show to send *him* into a therapist's office.

Dating Is Work

Think of the first few dates as classic job interviews. This is a time when all prospective employees are on their best behavior. In business you know the requirements—appropriate attire, punctuality, polite small talk, a keen interest in the company to which one is applying.

So why do women go out with a guy a second time if on the first date he wears jeans to a nice restaurant (or a nice suit to a casual place), if he shows up too late or too early, if he isn't a great conversationalist, and talks only about himself asking very little about you? I can hear the high-pitched cries right now. "But he was tall, he was gorgeous, he had a great job, he had such potential!" I wish I could have a pair of Kenneth Coles for every time I fell in love with someone's potential. Remember, potential can't love you back.

Thankfully, help is here. I have put together a foolproof list of perfect boyfriend behaviors. It's a handy checklist that helps you stay focused when your head is spinning, your heart is pounding, and your lower half is exploding. Perhaps more important, it includes a list of dating signposts that read "Dump Him Now!" I hope this will save a lot of women a lot of heartache.

This is not a list of Rules that tell you how to entice a man, thus blaming yourself when it doesn't work out. This is a list of acceptable male behaviors that will enable you to entice the *right* man.

The Boyfriend Test Can Change the World

I have a grandiose delusion about my ability to effect global change. Allow me that privilege, fellow girls' club member. I think *The Boyfriend Test* will also help men. A few symbolic slaps in the face can cause ripples throughout sports bars and locker rooms everywhere, and might bring about an adjustment in the behavior of the entire species. Who knows? My mother taught me to think big.

And grand change starts with one person. You. Followed soon after by the next man you meet. It works like this: We are known for what we accept as much as for what we reject. And by learning to dump the rejects, you are conversely inviting good behavior into your world. If enough women do this, that is, change the rules to read "Men must behave or be banished," then I think a relationship revolution is possible.

I learned that we sometimes unconsciously give permission to men's bad behavior during one of those horribly painful moments called a reality check. I was sitting in the bathtub one Christmas Day crying because I had been stood up for Midnight Mass the night before. Yes, you read it right. I was abandoned on one of the holiest nights of the year by a guy whose hurtful behavior wasn't even kept in check by a fear of burning in hell.

Granted, you have no reason to feel sorry for me. For the previous eighteen months I had ignored all the signs that this man was a poster boy for irresponsibility. He hid behind answering machines, showed up late to every event, refused to meet my friends—the usual commitment-phobic antics that seem to turn on so many women. Did I mention that he was a six-foot-four, blue-eyed, biracial babe who made women of all races drop to their knees at first sight? Unfortunately, I found out too late that women of all races were *literally* dropping to their knees for him...in his apartment, in his office, even in his car. You get the picture.

Anyway, back to my tearful tub scene. When he called with his usual words of contrition and apologies (think Academy Award material), I begged him to tell me why he treated me so badly. Why would he take so long to return my phone calls? Why would he disappear for days after I felt we'd gotten closer by making love? And in answer to my quivering queries came the most stone-cold honest answer a girl could ever ask for. "Because you let me," he said. With that I placed the receiver down and called AT&T to request a new number.

Two years later I was having dinner with a man further up the ladder in emotional maturity and he interrupted me while I was in full swing about the social ramifications of global awareness or some similar subject. "I never realized how smart you were," he said. "I had a weird impression of you because I had heard you went out with [the Christmas Eve guy]." His statement stunned me.

See, guys know what's up. And they think we're stupid for falling for bad behavior. In my case, great guys were avoiding me because I was sending out bad-girl signals. And that's what got me thinking about a cultural revolution. Imagine if we all, en masse, rejected bad boys and bad behavior. How would those men be able to reproduce? They wouldn't. They would have to change their ways or go the way of the dinosaur.

It's the law of natural selection. Female choice has been a huge determinant of the direction any species takes. Why else do male peacocks have such a show of colorful plumage? For no reason other than to attract mates. In days gone by, enough women chose colorful-feathered husbands who begot colorful sons. Voilà, the gorgeous peacock that we know today—created by female choice.

See, *The Boyfriend Test can* change the world. (Or, just as importantly, the world of one woman—you.)

Firing a loser makes room for a qualified man to enter your life. I promise you this works. Psychologists call it setting personal boundaries. New Age enthusiasts call it changing your energy signals. I'm more pragmatic. Dump the jerks. Date a better man. Period. Just do it.

PART A

TEST
yourself

When I tell people that I am writing a book called *The Boyfriend Test,* I get two common reactions. Women almost always cheer at the thought of putting men to the test, and men seem to take great offense at the thought. With both responses, I am quick to follow up with the comment that the first third of the book is actually a kind of *girlfriend* test. I wouldn't dream, I tell them, of evaluating anyone's emotional maturity until I had looked at my own issues. And that's what I'm about to ask you to do.

If you're an average single woman today, you probably have a career (or are on your way to one), you probably have a circle of friends, and your family fits somewhere in your life. All these relationships may have an effect on how you relate to men.

It's really important that we take the time to look inside ourselves and sift through the jigsaw puzzle of personality pieces to understand why we do what we do.

welcome to the girls' club

> Well, one thing you can say for masturbation...you certainly don't have to look your best.
> —Mart Crowley, *The Boys in the Band*

If you're reading this book, you probably already have some perception of the coveted place you hold in the estrogen alliance. I'll go one further and make it clear. You are a woman. The survival of your gender—and indeed your species—has always been dependent on a complex network of other women as supporters, confidantes, and protectors. Anthropologists who study the animal kingdom observe that females, because of small body size and dependent youngsters, are often vulnerable to the violence of marauding males. With chimpanzees (with whom we share 98 percent of our DNA), for example, rape is common, as is infanticide. The saving grace for a female is her mother, sisters, aunts, cousins, and friends. Elaborate systems of female bonds are the infrastructure that keep women and children safe.

So welcome to the girls' club, a safe place to be, but one wrought with tremendous responsibility. Full-fledged members of the girls' club are self-directed, confident women who don't dump all their values every time a buffed male enters the picture. In fact, I myself once mused whether we even need men at all.

For many moons, my career women friends and I mulled over that ultimate question: Why do we need a man?

I mean, we all know needy friends who *need* a relationship. But us? We are liberated women. We have achieved freedom and independence that our grandmothers only dreamed of. We have great jobs, cool apartments, spa days, car leases, Title IX, StairMaster butts, 401(k)s, and safe sex. Why give half of this up to an instant partner who might run off with both our loot *and* our heart?

The more we pondered this question, the more we realized that we had indeed finally reached full equality with the boys—and we, too, were now complete commitment-phobics.

Of course, the big reason to have a relationship, according to the media, was something called a biological clock. That one made me feel queasy. Is this a vital organ I should have? If you put your ear to my womb, you might hear gurgles from last night's apple crepe or pangs for my next nonfat latté, but you certainly wouldn't hear the tick of a Timex.

In whispered tones, my girls' club partners and I shared this news in steam rooms and on the sidelines at baby showers. Some of us felt unfeminine. I remember one office shower where two hours of perfectly good gossip time was spent debating the merits of cloth diapers over disposable. This was a touchy subject in California, where used disposable diapers apparently stay in the environment longer than breast implants. But the water shortage made all that washing of cloth diapers very politically incorrect. What was a well-meaning mom to do? The conversation was enough to make me create some business emergency and run to my car phone. I just didn't care. Neither did many of my friends. Were we missing out on maternal urges that forecasted the future bliss of the diaper dilemma?

Okay, I admit it. From time to time, a few of us did indeed whine about an internal cramp that would only be relieved by the caress of tiny hands. I noticed that the more evolved members of this group just went ahead and made a baby— alone. And they took full responsibility for it. One woman I met even went to a sperm bank to avoid any future confrontations with a man yearning to play ball with an offspring. And one of my friends satisfied her urge in the really brave and socially conscious way: She adopted an abused child.

All this gave way to a new thought. If a biological clock did exist, it seems the alarm shut-off button isn't necessarily found in a relationship. We can make a baby without a man.

Surprise, surprise. In fact, if technology continues to grow the way it has, we may soon be able to clone an infant and not suffer stretch marks after all. So again I put the question to my girls' club: Why do we need a relationship?

This time my single friends responded by extolling the virtues of paternal input. Their desire: to hold court in a "traditional" family. I'm not exactly sure what a traditional family is or what the benefit is of having one. What I do know is that Murphy Brown's baby isn't a product of one and Ted Kaczynski is.

My girlfriends claimed they'd like someone who could help with the diapers, carve the roast, and play hoops with their child. I sucked in my breath and quickly shot back, "So I'll hire a diaper service, remain a vegetarian, and tune in to the WNBA." Besides, if a relationship is akin to living with a male nanny, I have plenty of childless gay friends who would gladly volunteer for the privilege of answering to the moniker of "Daddy." And they wouldn't leave the toilet seat up! The last thing I want is life with a man whose primary function in my household is that of Mr. Mom.

And even if we did want a Mr. Mom, they're scarce. Lest you think troops of liberated straight men exist outside of the movies, hear this: I once sat in a hair salon enduring my usual two hours of foils and bleach (do blondes really have more fun or just more time on their hands?), and I overheard two divorced women exchanging war stories about single motherhood. I jumped in with words of condolence for the loss of male support in their household, and I was immediately met with a startling rebuff. Almost in unison they cried, "Oh, my life was much worse when I had *two* children to nurture!"

Point taken. Okay, then, what about companionship? Don't all those studies say that married and cohabiting people live longer than members of the lonely hearts club? Apparently human DNA doesn't do well in isolation.

But who's isolated? In this century, most urban working women seem less inclined to come down with an acute case of loneliness and more apt to be stricken with "friend buildup." It's one side effect of a hectic schedule, and it's characterized by a chronic clogging of voice mail and e-mail with messages left by acquaintances you guiltily don't have time to call. And as far as I know, you can wash a man right out of your hair, but there's not a shampoo around that can wipe out "friend buildup." No, loneliness rarely exists anymore, and it's not a reason to get hitched.

And even if we did decide to settle for one human to occupy our personal spaces on a permanent basis, wouldn't we rather choose someone with shared interests? Perhaps someone whose definition of the final four is the last four reps in a step class. Someone whose natural inclination is to, say, choose a chick flick over an action blockbuster. In a word, why wouldn't we choose a *chick?*

Now you are thinking that I've really lost my marbles. I forgot for a moment that most of my gal pals are probably straight rather than gay. And while we may not walk through life with a constant urge to reproduce in the biological sense, many of us dream of reproducing our last earth-shattering orgasm. And that feat may require a penis, a pair of strong hands, some firm buns...you get the picture.

Of course, a full-on *relationship* isn't necessary for sex. Just ask any guy. And thanks to the Pill, sex no longer has to be a family-oriented sport. Thanks to condoms, we no longer have to buy life insurance before each encounter (although it's a good idea to get a medical history on the dude anyway). And thanks to e-mail, after sex we no longer even have to talk to the penis again.

So there I was, back to square one. Why do we women need a relationship in twenty-first-century America? Not for financial security. Not for our biological clocks. Not for a Mr. Mom. Not for companionship. And certainly not for sex.

To pursue this further, I picked up a textbook left over from college. The course was called Sociology of the Family. In it I learned that way back in our evolutionary beginnings women didn't have one-on-one, monogamous relationships with members of the opposite sex. *Homo sapiens* in those days were hunters and gatherers, and our primary occupation was roaming the plains in groups, searching for food. (That was before drive-through McDonald's.) Women hung out together nurturing children. Men roamed the perimeter pro-tecting the flock. Men didn't much care about offspring unless one got big enough to challenge them and steal all the cute girls. Then they had a fight—a brutal, unsocialized fight like the famous one between Tyson and Holyfield. In those days life went like this: When people were hungry, they hunted; when they were horny, they humped. No questions asked.

Then something changed. We evolved from being a hunting-and-gathering society to an agriculture-based one. Yes, we became farmers before we became trailer-park trash. This, according to my college professor, was the greatest downfall of the female gender. You see, along with farming came the accumulation of stuff. Suddenly men owned a piece of dirt, a hut, some tools, maybe even a McKeda drill. And when they grew old, the thought suddenly arose that maybe they'd like to leave this stuff with someone when they died. So they chose offspring. And the only way to determine who your offspring were was to confine a woman, giving way to the barefoot-and-pregnant-in-the-kitchen ideal.

The industrial revolution that came a few thousand years later didn't help much. Suddenly the procurement of food was based on money, and the only way to get money was to do work that was labor intensive. Read: You needed big muscles to get a job and buy food, and you needed an abundance of testosterone to build big muscles. So we women were out of luck again. Our survival was dependent on hitching up with some cousin of a Neanderthal who could hold down a job and buy Twinkies for our kids. Yuck!

These were the social conditions that led our great-grandmothers and grandmothers, and maybe even our mothers, to stay in unhappy relationships. Survival of the fittest, it's called. No wonder. You had to be fit to survive many of those relationships.

Thankfully, we have continued to evolve. Over the last century we've entered the technological age. Most jobs these days are not labor intensive. Theoretically, both women and men have equal opportunity to punch keyboards, fly jets, and take meetings with smarmy attorneys, all in the name of making money to buy food and stuff. Heck, women can even be the smarmy attorney! Work has nothing to do with muscles. We're finally free. And we can go back to nurturing in girl packs. When we're hungry, we can make reservations. When we're horny, we can make booty calls. Hurrah for Darwin!

But (and you knew there'd be a but) there is a catch. If this is true, if we can really go back to our unconscious meandering in search of bagels and bodies, why are we spending so much time reading self-help books and fretting over relationship questions? The answer to that one is a little complex: because we are no longer unconscious.

We've evolved biologically. We've evolved sociologically. We've evolved mentally, and we've evolved spiritually. We now have a conscience. The more evolved our brains are, the more we are aware of our actions, our aspirations, our happiness, and our connections to others.

And we understand cause and effect. For instance, a hunter-gatherer probably had no idea that inserting his penis into a woman's body would cause her to get pregnant. He had an itch, so he scratched it. Today we know that spreading our legs for a man can cause yeast infections, chlamydia gonorrhea, herpes, AIDS, and yes, conception. It can also cause plenty of hurt feelings if we want to do it a second time and he doesn't, or vice versa. We also know that kids from two-parent families have a greater chance for success.

A hunter-gatherer only knew that food would cure a pain in his stomach. We now know that how we eat can make us healthy or sick. In fact, we've gone past making enough money just to buy food and instead have tried to satisfy our hunger with houses, and cars, and Prada bags, and we've learned that they don't satisfy us. We also know that dozens of e-mail messages don't equate to even one meaningful relationship.

All this came to me during that lengthy stint of reading and researching. My parents had just died and my gazillionth relationship had just failed. Answering this psychological wake-up call, I moved to a new apartment, changed my phone number, unplugged the television set, and began to consider my position in the world.

In the end, I discovered that I didn't need a relationship at all. In fact, very few women in our modern culture need a relationship to survive or to reproduce.

But that's not the point. I came to realize that our mission in life is not simply to reproduce. Our mission is to evolve. And for that we need stimulation. Mental stimulation, emotional stimulation, spiritual stimulation, and even sexual stimulation. Fortunately, it all comes packaged in one attractive container called a man. Men can be a Rubik's Cube for the soul and a Nautilus machine for the mind, and even a soothing steam room when life gets too cold. Simply put, a relationship can help us grow.

In interpersonal relationships, there's something invigorating about the clash of mismatched hormones laced with love and respect. An emotionally intimate, intellectually stimulating, sexually charged relationship provides an opportunity for personal growth that no other life experience can match. A real relationship is so daunting that it's downright scary. But we have to keep trying.

On the following pages you will find a specific plan on where to meet, how to greet, and how to choose the man who can be your match. He is a man who is smart enough to attempt the kind of evolution you need. Go for it, girlfriend!

your test

> So many women are determined to understand what makes the liar tick. Why not focus instead on why they suspended their own good sense and reasonable doubt to believe him?
>
> —Dr. Dory Hollander,
>   *101 Lies Men Tell Women*

It's easy to complain that there are no great men around. And it's all too convenient (and fun) to tell horror stories about nightmare dates and old loser boyfriends to prove the point that all men are jerks. But what's difficult is to look toward ourselves for the reason we lust after losers.

Before we begin a psychological look in the mirror, please take comfort in this fact: Everybody has bad relationships. Many people have had many, many bad relationships. In truth, it is only a lucky few who have squeaked through adolescence and early adult life unscathed by romantic love. Even the father of modern therapy, Sigmund Freud, knew of heartbreak. In *Civilization and Its Discontents,* he wrote, "We are never so defenseless against suffering as when we love." So the bottom line is you're not alone if you've ever sobbed into your pillow over some cute slob with a deep voice.

Breakups are nearly inevitable because serial relationships are the way of modern society. And that's not altogether a bad thing. Unlike our grandmothers, who may have stayed in godawful, emotionally repressive or damaging relationships, we have the ability to shop for a more appropriate penis when one gets us down. (That doesn't mean, of course, that we always should. I'll get to that in a minute.)

The trick is to upgrade your man with each relationship and improve your own ability to deal with him. That's evolution. Each new love affair is a revealing growth experience. We learn something new about ourselves and the opposite sex. Each new relationship brings us closer to our Dream Man, because we learn how to spot him and how to behave toward him.

A stable, loving, long-term relationship is a work of art. Do you think Michelangelo's first swish with a paintbrush was at the Sistine Chapel? Hardly. I'm sure he had to learn and practice on his way to perfection. So you should expect to have a heap of old loves who taught you how to be a better girlfriend and, just as important, how to choose a better boyfriend.

With that said, I should add that just because we can fire a loser anytime we want doesn't mean we should. A new relationship won't make you any happier if you're the same person entering into it. That's the catch. You have to become a better girlfriend each time around.

I once heard the expression that happiness isn't something you find in a relationship. Happiness is "baggage" you must carry in with you. The idea confused me. In all my fondest dreams and Cinderella stories, men provided happiness. I thought a wonderful man would somehow complete me.

In my case it took a few wonderful men to show me that that isn't true. Wonderful men have bad days. Wonderful men sometimes forget to tell their partner they're beautiful. Wonderful men sometimes have Laker fever and disappear during the play-offs. Wonderful men sometimes lose their job, or their temper, or their hair. And a lot of the time, wonderful men are just that, wonderful. But on his off days some self-esteem and optimism on your part go a long way toward dealing with Mr. Wonderful.

Now, if I had all the answers on how to attain personal happiness, you would probably have a holiday on my birthday. What I do know is that the world is set up backwards. When you wish you had a boyfriend, you find yourself home too many nights watching reruns of *I Love Lucy* on Nick at Night and worrying about the *Glamour* magazine "Don't's" that you "Did." And just when you hit on some days of frivolous utopia where your work, your friends, and your hobbies bring you joy, your cell phone blasts with calls from men that somehow now seem like an interruption in your very full life. Go figure.

Think about your life as a thriving company that might consider a merger if it was mutually beneficial to both firms. Your company shouldn't be looking for a bailout. Now, with that concept in mind, consider what goes into building a healthy business—things like a smart business plan, fiscal strength, a good public image, for starters.

Add to that consistent supply delivery and strong leadership. Now think about how all these apply to your life.

Do you really know what you want? Are you punctual and do you show people respect by returning their phone calls on time? Or are you a bit of a flake? Do you have financial debt? Do you practice strong values or just search for them? Do you have discipline? In short, are *you* good girlfriend material?

M. Scott Peck wrote in his classic best-seller, *The Road Less Traveled,* "If being loved is your goal, you will fail to achieve it. The only way to be assured of being loved is to be a person worthy of love, and you cannot be a person worthy of love if your primary goal is to passively be loved."

Of course, we would all like to *think* we are the perfect girlfriend, but unless we look at our own foibles and follies, we will never be able to accept them in others. Unless we practice good behavior, we can't expect it from others.

One man I know, an architect in his midthirties, told me he is wildly attracted to women who are independent and have their own direction in life, but too often he finds that women only "pretend" to be those things. As an example, he told me he once went on a date with an actress in her late twenties who exhibited all the signs of success: a nice car, the ability to get a good table at restaurants, and platinum American Express card. She appeared to have a good head on her shoulders, and while she wasn't a movie star, she had a blossoming career.

After the date, she brought him back to her well-appointed condo. While she was in the bathroom, he noticed many photos displayed of her with older men who appeared well below her level in the looks department. Of course, there's a chance they all had big hearts and attractive brains, so my friend didn't immediately jump to conclusions. However, when he quizzed her about the men in the photos, she referred to them as ex-boyfriends and quickly gave a rundown of their net worth. My friend couldn't wait to run from that apartment. Here was a women parading independence yet appeared to be riding the purse strings of a bunch of older benefactors.

The next week this same male friend went out with a woman who drove a late-model but well-maintained car and lived in a small but nicely decorated rental unit. After clearly outlining her plans to get to the next level in business, she added that she struggled with the issue of how to fit in marriage and family, but was sure the man she chose would help her in her balancing act. My friend almost had his knees buckle over that one. Here was a woman who was very clear that she was the one doing the choosing! This man immediately felt the challenge to live up to her expectations. It was obvious she knew what she wanted, and he liked that. Today, they live together and both work from home so they can share parenting responsibilities of their newborn son.

So think hard about your life before you begin to sort through that haystack. Are you searching for a glistening needle or grasping for straws to add to your straw house?

Put Yourself to the Girlfriend Test

Mirror, mirror on the wall, tell me my foibles, tell them all. It's time, oh fair women friends, to really see if we are ready for a relationship. Here are some questions that must be put to you before you can go on the offense and begin to test the men you meet. There are no quick answers to these soul-searching queries, so I suggest you take a day or so and spend some downtime turning over each one.

QUESTION #1

Are Your Career Conflicts Resolved? Whether you're wavering on what to do or wrapped up in a power job, your career may affect your ability to have a relationship.

Career Conflict Number One: You're Still Not Sure Exactly What You Want to Do or Who You Want to Be

Our nine-to-five life is such an important part of our identity. Our jobs can provide creative gratification, self-esteem, money, and independence—all personal rewards that our boyfriends should *not* be responsible for. If you're still undecided about your aspirations and your life is at a creative crossroads, there's a strong possibility that you will unconsciously choose a shoulder to lean on rather than a partner to lie down with.

When I was twenty-something and still on the "six-year B.A. plan" (read: I wasn't sure what I wanted to do, so I kept taking time from school to explore my options), I found myself in a number of different business settings. Because I was young, impressionable, and eager to plan my future, I fell into a few relationships with bosses and mentoring coworkers. (That was long before sexual harassment laws made bosses more wary of who they dated.) With each of these relationships I truly believed that I had found a perfect boyfriend. Unfortunately, though, those romantic liaisons tended to fall apart when I developed a distaste for the particular field of employment. In other words, I had little in common with those men other than my newfound interest in their business. At the time I was oblivious to the fact. In my heart, I really felt it was pure love. Are you listening, Ms. Lewinsky? In my case, I needed a decade of hindsight to prove myself wrong.

This might be a good place to add that your career aspiration may be to be the best mother in the world, or as one friend of mine calls herself, a "specialist in early-childhood education." That's perfectly fine. As women we're allowed to choose the hardest job on earth if we want to. But then please admit it to yourself! And if you can, take some child psychology classes while you're working at whatever job occupies your time until your "career" happens.

Moreover, don't be afraid to admit this to the boyfriend candidates you are testing. I promise there are as many men out there who want a loving wife and mother (for their kids!) as there are men looking for a babe with a paycheck.

Not only can your business setting influence your romantic targets, but if you're unsure of who you are, your romance may influence your job selection. The women I meet who appear to be most in conflict are the ones who seem to transform themselves, including their jobs, to suit the men they're dating. I know one thirty-three-year-old woman about to enter her fourth marriage who has been a dental hygienist, an actress, and a clothing designer, all tailored to suit the tastes of her husband of the moment—a dentist, a producer, and a garment manufacturer! Of course, she's never been successful in any of those ventures because she wasn't doing them to satisfy her own passion. Recently she told me that her true aspiration is to be a wife and mother, and it is her latest fiancé who has brought this to her attention. I'm suspicious again.

While her case is extreme, ponder this: I believe that in our culture women are raised to cooperate while men are raised to compete. If you find yourself switching careers and men often, ask yourself, honestly, how much your career choice is designed to meet a man or please a man.

Of course, no one feels completely settled all the time. Life is one big journey of connected transitions. But having some kind of self-generated stability can go a long way toward saving your heart in a romantic collision.

Career Conflict Number Two: Your Job Comes First

Having a career and a healthy relationship is the most delicate balancing act next to having a career and children. To put it in perspective, having a boyfriend and a career is sometimes like getting a manicure while you talk on a cell phone. One part of your mind loves being pampered and the other is trying to preserve your nails and maintain the cell signal. A great job can provide us with self-esteem and independence, but it can't do everything for our soul. As I said in Chapter 1, we still need a romantic relationship to sustain our growth.

Here's one exercise to do: Visualize having a perfect boyfriend. You'll learn how to create him in the next chapter, but for now focus on one dazzling hero who got away. Now, imagine that you've just been given a dream job, the one you've always wanted, complete with title and salary hike. Next, assume the boyfriend is entrenched in a career in your current city and your dream job is in Anchorage. If the first thing you wonder is whether a down parka can look fashionable with the right pair of boots, you've lost points on the girl-friend scale.

Okay, okay. I hear the roar of my sister feminists right now: But if he's a great guy, he would understand! He would either move with me for such a wonderful opportunity, or he would meet me at romantic halfway points until I returned.

The truth is that relationships that work well when partners live in close proximity rarely survive long distance. The dynamics and pressures are very different. The reverse is also true. If you happened to meet Mr. Right on a business trip to Anchorage and have been having a wonderful AT&T/Alaska Air relationship, there's a very good chance that things wouldn't be so cozy if you moved into his igloo.

But the bigger issue here is your inability to even *imagine* choosing a relationship over a career. In truth, you may in fact meet a great guy who is willing to switch jobs and move with you, or you may become a couple where *his* job is more crucial to your mutual financial or lifestyle goals. But you have to be prepared to adjust.

Some other questions to ask yourself are: Would you automatically cancel a date if a business appointment comes up? Or do you always cancel a business event if a hot man calls? The answers to those questions might signal that you're on a never-ending seesaw between career and relationships, rather than striking a balance.

I know from whence I speak, for I was once in superpower career mode myself. There was a year where I was anchoring the news in Los Angeles, hosting a show on HBO, and working as the entertainment correspondent for the *Weekend Today Show* on NBC—all at the same time! That year I worked exactly 365 days. No joke.

During that time I also squeezed in dozens of dates. Besides running myself ragged, I was truly too busy and too focused on my professional life to have a real relationship with anybody. I'm sure I bruised a few male egos with my last-minute cancellations, long games of phone tag, and hasty departures from dinner tables, all in the name of covering a hot story and getting on air, but I didn't feel I had a choice. For me it took a year off from all romance and a lengthy period of celibacy to clear my head and start over. (I'll tell you more about that in the final chapter of this book.) My biggest regret about my life during that time was that I spent endless hours complaining that most of the men I was seeing refused to get emotionally intimate, yet I wasn't even being in touch with my own emotions! I was distracted by my hectic life.

Today I balance my romantic, family, work, and personal lives with a bit of modern technology: my computer scheduler. When I enter appointments or tasks, I give them different color typefaces that correspond with the various areas of my life. For example, events and to-do's that concern my daughter are pink (she's soft and cute). Those that pertain to television are green (they pay me money). My relationship and personal "Wendy time" are highlighted in royal purple (I'm a queen in my own mind). And my creative writing pursuits are urgently typed in red letters (deadlines are pressure). When I glance at my computer, I can tell immediately by the way the colors bathe the screen, whether I am in balance. (This week, by the way, there's a lot of pink and not enough green.)

You can do the same thing with a paper schedule and some highlighter pens. Look clearly at your life and see if you've made room for a healthy relationship.

Are Your Business Life and Your Personal Tastes at Odds?

Some other things to consider regarding career and relationships: Do your romantic inclinations gel with your schedule? You may work nights in the restaurant industry but seem to be attracted to Wall Street brokers who are at their desks by seven. May I remind you that relationships take time. Plenty of in-your-face kind of time. Unless you plan on having bags under your eyes forever, you may want to rethink your romantic target.

Or are your business life and your personal picks at odds? Let's say you favor longhaired musicians even though the conservative law firm where you work requires you and your significant other to attend plenty of social functions. While I don't think the primary function of your man should be social arm piece, if you love your career and want to get ahead, you might choose a man whose nine-to-five has more synergy with yours.

So before you consider test-driving a boyfriend, you have to know your direction in life. If you are stuck in your career's fast lane or keep taking wrong turns, you may find yourself driving lemons.

Do You Have a Grown-Up Rapport with Mom and Dad? If you're still your parents' daughter rather than your own woman, it's time to graduate to a big-girl bed.

In her book *The 10 Smartest Decisions a Woman Can Make Before 40*, Tina Tesina says a big indicator of the role you play with your parents is the names you call them. If they are still "Mommy" and "Daddy," it's time to stop! (That is, of course, if you are potty-trained and out of a high chair.)

Sometimes our childish behavior with our parents (or even siblings) is so subtle that we don't realize that we are trapped in infantile tendencies that affect our ability to have a mature relationship with the right man. Many of us, even way into adulthood, function as family people-pleaser or rebel without realizing we are doing it.

This notion dawned on me a few years ago with my parents' deaths. That awful life-altering tragedy turned out to be the greatest gift of self-discovery. My psychological umbilical cord was instantly snapped, and after much grieving, I chose to figure out what was causing so much pain.

The day after my mother's funeral, I returned to work as a

news anchor, and when I looked into the camera that evening, a long-forgotten little voice inside my soul asked, "What is this for? Why am I doing this? Mom can't be my fan now." I realized that a decade after college I was still making career decisions based on the need for my mother's approval!

In the relationship realm, I discovered that I was seeking quite the opposite of approval. A year after Mom passed, my father died. (Cancer is a bitch! Please eat well, exercise, and don't smoke.) Soon after, I looked into the eyes of the hoodlum in my bed and that same little voice announced, "Oooh! Dad would hate this guy. But now it doesn't matter."

Before their deaths, I had no idea that many of my life choices were designed to either piss off or please my parents. Deep down, at the age of thirty-two, I was still partly a struggling teenager.

So, short of hiring a hit on your most beloved, how do you take a realistic look at your parental ties and determine if they are secretly sabotaging your girlfriend potential?

Assess the Parent Factor

Start by adding up how much of your head space your parents occupy. Calculate how much time you spend talking to, visiting with, thinking about, or talking about your original family. Check your phone bill and your frequent-flyer miles. Listen to your language. Do you mention them often, even in angry or complaining ways? How often are they a factor in your life or plans?

Ask close friends for their opinion about your family connections. (Note: Solicit only Friends, with a capital *F*, not acquaintances or hangers-on. I define true friends as those individuals who you can call at two A.M. in an emergency or who will drive you to the airport.)

Of course, time alone may not be the only indicator of healthy or unhealthy family connections. One girlfriend of mine swears her mom is not a factor in her boyfriend drought. She supports this claim by saying she only sees her mother for Sunday-night dinners and never talks about her male relationships. As background information, you should know that my friend's mom is divorced, doesn't date, and politely waits for any crumb of info on her daughter's life so that she can live through it.

Well, I attended one of those Sunday-night dinners and have an outsider's report. Mom was busy trying to win her daughter's favor by laying out a fab home-cooked meal and fussing over her adult child's every whim. My friend, on the other hand, spent her psychological energy trying to deflect her mom's attentions by ignoring her, giving one-word answers, or staring at the television. From my view I saw a codependent relationship where one tried to overlove and the other resented it all.

My friend, when asked to consider it, admits that maybe she doesn't talk to her mother about dating because a part of her brain doesn't want to hurt her mother's feelings. After all, if my friend really did get a boyfriend, she'd be abandoning Mom. And that contributes to her unconscious resentment.

Granted, having a loving and supportive family you are close to isn't in itself a boyfriend deterrent. But an immature,

unhealthy relationship with them can be. For starters you'll
end up repeating the bad behavior in your love relationship.
So find a way, either through professional psychotherapy,
counseling, or independent soul-searching, to step outside
your family for a while and get a good look at how they (and
you!) operate.

Are You Running from a Bad Relationship, a Dead-End Job, or a Biological Clock? These are three good reasons to have a loving relationship with yourself before you cast your poor victimized soul on a man.

We have all met someone on the rebound. Running from a
bad relationship seems to be a constant state of being for
some of my friends. One girlfriend of mine jumps from relationship to relationship as if she's on a trampoline secured by
her heartstrings. It seems like every month she's fallen head-
over-heels for another perfect man. After each breakup, she
medicates herself with wine, dinner, and new sex. But she's
getting no closer to discovering her true inner desires, nor is
she truly healing.

Another girlfriend of mine hates her job. She says it's unin-
spiring and creatively ungratifying. She doesn't leave it

because she's afraid to take a financial risk. So she directs all her energy toward dating and finding a soul mate who might rescue her from her dead-end job.

Eggs are the focus of another friend—lack of eggs, to be precise. Her biological clock is ticking as she turns thirty-eight this year. Apparently the average woman is born with about four hundred little suckers neatly tucked in her ovaries. On average we drop about one a month for thirty-six years. Unlike men, who flow like the Amazon River for eighty years, at some point our booty bottoms out and the eggs stop a-comin'. That basic reality of feminine life has my friend chasing sperm through bars and restaurants and down office hallways like they're the last candy bar on Planet PMS.

All three of these women have the same problem. Fear. In these cases it is fear of being alone, fear of being trapped forever in a dead-end job, and fear of being a childless woman. By the way, the answer to each of these problems is simply not a man!

These women's anxieties have limited their patience and are spoiling relationships before they begin. And theirs aren't the only fears that get in the way of relationship contentment. Some women fear the relationship itself! There are bookshelves of professional advice for women like these, but I have some girlfriend wisdom.

First calm your mind. Check out of popular culture. Turn off all TVs, phones, and stereos. Light a candle. Sit quietly. Take about forty deep breaths. Cry if you need to. Then calmly finish this sentence: My biggest relationship fear is...

It could be fear of abandonment, fear of losing control, fear of growing old alone, fear of missing out on motherhood, fear of emotional or physical abuse, fear of the loss of financial independence, fear of breakups, fear of inheriting someone else's financial mess, fear of the pain of infidelity, or even fear of getting fat by sharing decadent dinners every night. You name it. If you're a neurotic chick like me, you can dream up any fear to keep you out of a good relationship.

In the next few weeks, closely examine your answers and become aware of how they relate to your behavior. Yes, document your behavior to see if it affects your dating IQ. Make a chart if you like. List all the men you've recently dated or flirted with, and add each new man as you meet him. Make notes about how quickly you return their calls, what hours you take their calls, and how available you are. Now add to that list how apt they are, in your opinion, to make one of your fears a reality.

I know a woman who fits the description of a classic child of alcoholics. Her dad, after being physically abusive toward her mother, left when she was ten. Her adult life has been riddled with two kinds of relationships: lengthy ones with older, controlling men, and short ones with men whom she tries to control. Her brain is probably working this way: *First I'll try to duplicate my daddy. He'll be mean like my father, but if I'm really "good" to him, maybe he won't leave me.* Her hope in this situation is to assume the control she lacked as a child. When that kind of unhealthy relationship disintegrates, she opts for another unhealthy approach: *I'll never let anyone hurt me like that again, I'll find a "nice" guy who I can control. I'll make sure he can't hurt me.* Of course, as we all know, most men don't take too kindly to being controlled, so those turn out to be her shortest relationships.

My friend entered therapy in the last few years and has begun to see these self-deprecating patterns. Just illuminating our issues is often enough to cause great change. In my humble girlfriend opinion, I think she's choosing much better boyfriend candidates these days.

Looking at your chart, you should watch for two kinds of behaviors. Obviously, take notice if you are often very available to men who will help you realize your biggest fears. But also watch for retreats from men who don't satisfy your fears and probably leave because you are subconsciously rejecting them for their healthy behavior. They are both signs that you may unconsciously be looking to create a dysfunctional relationship. Once your dysfunction is out of the closet, it will make change a little easier. My favorite country and western song about this phenomenon is called "If You Won't Leave Me, I'll Find Someone Who Will."

Finally, consult Chapter 3 to help you to determine a set of compatible traits that will keep you focused on finding a realistic relationship, rather than a salve for your aching psyche.

An old friend of mine was the baby of her family. Her father flew the coop way too early: when she was two years old. She was raised by a loving mother and older sisters and brothers who fiercely protected her. However, in their love and protection, her family may have unconsciously programmed her to fear men. Her mother would say things like, "Honey, your father wasn't that bad of a guy. At least he didn't beat us." What a message, Ma! So, the rest of the guys *beat* women, too?

As you can imagine, my friend sent out cold energy to both kinds of men, the nice guys and the bad boys, until she began to understand her fears.

When I answered that "fear" question myself a few years back, I said my biggest relationship fear was that a man would leave me. I feared breakups more than relationships. Interestingly, I was also having more breakups than relationships. It was as if I invited in what I most feared.

Abandonment, as it turns out, is one of the most common human fears because, as infants, our lives are dependent on the fact that someone will stay near. Every time a mother walks out of a newborn's line of vision, her little bundle believes she's dead. Gone. Disappeared forever. So he or she lets out some tiny yelps until someone returns to comfort her. My own daughter got so good at this "game" that I barely put her down during her first year of life. In fact, infant psychologists today preach a strong attachment to a primary caregiver with brief separations led by a child's readiness, rather than the "cry-it-out" philosophy of yesterday.

For me to face up to my adult fear of abandonment, I had to delve into my childhood to see what extenuating circumstances made this fear so pronounced in me. Unlike many of my friends' parents, mine had stayed together, so I assumed I hadn't fallen prey to the "Abandoning Daddy Syndrome." Or had I? When I spent some time analyzing it, I determined that, as a repressed introvert, my father was at least emotionally unavailable, and he also had a job that literally forced him to abandon me for long stretches of time—he was in the navy.

The career he had chosen had him sailing the seven seas, and his homecomings were highlighted by little trinkets he brought back for me—castanets from Spain, a hula skirt from Hawaii. The biggest gift I ever received was a set of luggage. Fitting.

Throughout my twenties, my romantic inclinations tended toward distant men, either emotionally or physically. I "loved" long-distance relationships, where treks to LAX to pick up Mr. Right-This-Moment brought flashes of the little girl waiting on the dock to glimpse the tiny dot on the horizon that was my father's ship coming to port. The revelation about my unhealthy though familiar relationship patterns came to me as a news reporter during the Persian Gulf War. While I was hovering in a helicopter over a destroyer in Long Beach, California, to report on the safe homecoming of a crew, my visual radar kept picking up one little girl who stood staring as the gangplank was lowered. On our flight back to the station, I put on my sunglasses to conceal my tears from the camera crew.

Have You Dealt with Your Childhood Issues? Facing lingering issues and fears is only the beginning of a journey toward personal growth that will lead you to a happy relationship.

Here's a pessimistic, though too often true, statement: If you think you've had a happy childhood, you're in denial. The act of growing from completely dependent being to totally independent person is a painful one. The time you fell off the monkey bars, didn't get the part in the school play, were scolded by a teacher you respected, or jeered by the field hockey team, your psyche took a hit. It was a tiny hit and maybe you ignored it, but a part of your brain didn't forget it. Take twenty years of those kinds of hits and you build up some issues.

There is no better investment in your future than psychological therapy. Studies have shown that people can make courageous change through consistent, respectful therapy. Here's why:

Think of your brain as an iMac with a computer bug that causes it to freeze up with regularity. The bug was accidentally planted during early production. (Sorry, Macintosh, iMacs are exceptional computers, but a few of the early models *did* have problems.)

You have a choice. You can put up with a computer that

keeps stalling and spend way longer than you need to to get your work done, or you can take it to an expert to find the cause of the problem. Of course, if you choose not to take it to an expert, you risk a total computer crash and the loss of all your life's work.

One girlfriend of mine is a devout Catholic and had a great resistance to psychotherapy. In my opinion, the only way to be female, single, and Catholic nowadays is to ignore a few of the rules.

Anyway, at the age of thirty-four, my friend finally entered therapy. After only six months I can see the results. She's more aware, more conscious of her words and actions, and already she's choosing boyfriend candidates who are more appropriate for her. Despite her astounding results, therapy isn't a quick fix. It is a lifelong journey that may need to be embraced if we are to pass the Girlfriend Test. After all, how can we ask for an evolved boyfriend if we are not in the process of evolving ourselves?

Even Bad Emotions Make Us Feel Whole

Dr. Susan C. Vaughan, in her book *The Talking Cure,* makes this case for therapy:

> [It] works because it involves our experiencing of intense and often painful affects as they arise when we explore the past and the present. ...[S]eeing that we do not die or disintegrate

when we experience intense anger, anxiety, sadness, shame, or excitement gives us a growing capacity to experience emotions more fully while feeling more capable of modulating our emotional reactions....[As children] we may have had caretakers whose approach to teaching us self-restraint left us ashamed and humiliated, lacking the ability to repair a relationship—and our own self-esteem—once it ruptured. If so, then psychotherapy will help us feel less ashamed and less inhibited. We will begin to experience relationships as less fragile. Overall, our capacity for an expanded range of affects and our growing ability to regulate them will help to make the tapestry of our lives richer, brighter, and more pleasurable.

Simply put, after a bunch of bloodletting, heart-wrenching crying jags in a climate-controlled office with a trustworthy guide, you feel stuff more. Bad feelings aren't so scary. And good feelings are really, really good.

The first time I noticed this phenomenon, I was roasting in my jet-black car on a hot day in August. I was pissed off because I had just come out of a time-wasting meeting and was now forced to burn more time in a traffic jam. I was angry, but I wasn't crazy angry. I observed my angry state and was able to recognize that it was limited to two small events: the lost opportunity for business in my meeting, and the lost opportunity to spend an extra hour with my daughter due to being stuck in traffic. I mourned these losses and put them in perspective. And I didn't do my normal brain reflex: find things to hate about (a) my boyfriend, (b) my hairdresser, or (c) my complexion. Instead I just looked at the anger and said to myself, "Oh, this is what mad feels like."

When I got home, I quickly donned my shorts, scooped up my baby, and retreated to the garden. I can't begin to describe how good it all felt as I lay on the grass with my angel on my stomach. The air smelled super clean, my daughter's coos were the sweetest I'd ever heard, and my body was more calm and relaxed than I could ever remember. In days of old, I might still have been fuming over the traffic. Instead I found myself saying, "Ahhh. This is what happiness feels like." That adjustment in my psyche came after eighteen months in therapy, and I have continued on for many more years.

Shrinks Ain't Cheap, But They're Worth It

No doubt about it, one of the biggest deterrents to therapy is the hole it puts in your Kate Spade-like bag. Yes, therapy can be expensive, but almost every university that teaches psychiatry or psychology has a low-budget clinic staffed by graduates. While they may be students, they are graduate students, and for as little as five dollars an hour, you can be sitting across from a sympathetic listener. And you can shop a few schools or a few therapists to find the one you feel most comfortable with, emotionally and financially.

I have a male friend who was a struggling actor when he began therapy at UCLA's School of Psychiatry eighteen years ago. Back then he paid ten dollars for his sessions with a brilliant young, budding psychiatrist. Almost two decades later she has become a published author and he a huge Hollywood director. And they still have a standing weekly appointment! See? Therapy works.

Have You Clearly Defined Your Dream Relationship? If you can visualize it, then you can attain it.

As Kevin Costner's character learned in the film *Field of Dreams,* if you build it, they will come. This applies to boyfriends as well. What you have to build is a sturdy landing pad for your Dream Man to jump onto.

This is so important that I have devoted an entire chapter to the subject. Read on to Chapter 3 and I'll teach you a very pragmatic way to design a man to suit your needs. For now, just know that if you don't know what you're looking for, you will surely never find it.

Is Your Support Group "Supporting" Your Single Habit?

Sometimes our nearest and dearest can be quietly sabotaging our chances for a successful relationship and actually helping us stay single.

Whether it's the pack of women we run with or our big brothers, sisters, or mother, sometimes the people closest to us have a vested interest in keeping us single. The reality is that when we finally hunker down with a hunk, we'll likely abandon our current gang—at least for a while. And, when we come up for air from our postorgasm feather pillow, we may find a few friends with their noses out of joint.

This can be a touchy subject and one that's difficult to conceive. After all, most of us have wonderfully supportive friends whom we call, well, *friends*. And friends want friends to be happy, don't they? Well, up to a point, they do. But, contrary to popular mythology, it is much easier to survive a friend's sorrows than it is to survive her joys.

There are two reasons for this: First, underneath every loving friendship is an age-old reflex called female competition. And, until we consciously acknowledge this pesky throwback to the Stone Age, it'll work behind the scenes to sabotage our relationships. It's that green monster in our head that most women refuse to see. And the second reason we don't really want our friends to win love's lottery is because most of us fear change. Although change helps us grow, it can also be pretty painful, and the easier route is to simply work to maintain the status quo.

What makes this aspect of human dynamics confusing is that our girlfriends don't *pretend* to care about our heartbreaks. They truly do care. But on some level they also fear for their own emotional survival if we were to disappear into the tunnel of love.

I had a wonderful group of girlfriends who commiserated with me every time a man failed The Boyfriend Test. In fact, I had so many close girlfriends that one man whom I dated briefly told me later that part of our relationship problem was that he didn't feel he was dating me alone. He felt like he was dating a panel!

Point taken. But it was still many years before I noticed that whenever a man appeared to be a serious candidate for "Mr. Right" some of my friends convinced me he was "Mr. Wrong."

One woman in particular was the ultimate shoulder to lean on during my stays at the heartbreak hotel. She was so good at lifting my spirits. She was funny. She loved to party. And she was the champion of the get-back-on-the-horse-and-ride-it therapy. What I failed to see was that she liked me best when I was following her back to hell.

I discovered this when I told her about a wonderful man whom I had recently met. Her response: "I met him awhile ago at a wedding. I think he's too nice for you."

A few weeks later, while out with my new man, I saw her at a movie theater and she barely spoke to me. It was then that it dawned on me. *Of course* this man was "too nice" for me in her book. He actually had the potential to permanently take me off the single's market.

The moral of the story: No one can really know what you need besides you. Analyze your friends' motives before you take their advice.

Are You Attempting to Have Long-Term Relationships Using Short-Term Goals?
Tight skirts might get you a date, but only a quick mind will get you a boyfriend.

All dating is not intended to create a relationship. Ask any man who possesses those fleet-footed sperm that I've mentioned. But are there *women* out there who really want a fling rather than a flight down the aisle?

Sure there are. I've already mentioned women who unconsciously attract a fling by sabotaging their relationships out of fear. Their conscious mind claims they want long-term monogamy, but their unconscious steers them to something less fulfilling and shorter in duration.

Meanwhile, there are others who make a clear decision to opt for short-term relationships because of money, or lack of money. That's an anthropological truth. Some women in our culture look for help surviving in a world that can be financially unfair to women. And men sometimes equal resources.

For many generations, in fact, men were the *only* route to resources. And I'm not talking about prostitution, although hookers are an extreme example of what evolutionary psychologist David Buss calls "resource extraction."

What I mean is this. You gotta eat, right? Maybe you have babies to feed, too. You may not have the education or the self-confidence to survive in the formal workplace, so one of your options is men. If you're physically blessed, you might feel that short-term, serial relationships are easier than working. Professional girlfriends and wives-in-training are rarely talked about politely, but they do exist, and they work hard, for the kind of man who enters a resource-heavy cooperative with a woman usually exacts a high emotional wage.

Evolutionary psychologists pass no judgment on the practice of women seeking resource extraction from men. It is a simple fact of life that happens for distinct reasons, most often survival.

There are some clear dating strategies for women seeking a short-term relationship, and they most often have to do with flexible boundaries and suggestive attire. If you need evidence, just cruise by the doorway to any stadium locker room after the game. Short skirts and high heels are the standard uniform for hovering sports "groupies."

Do I have a problem with women who seek short-term relationships? Nope. In fact, I think the most extreme example, prostitution, should be legalized, taxed, have strict age requirements enforced, and workers should be eligible for state benefits. If some women believe that their body is their most profitable tool (even though the rest of us think differently), then let them use it. The only part of prostitution that I find unsettling are the men who control the industry. This includes pimps and the police officers who "allow" prostitutes to run their business in exchange for information about criminal activity. As in any other patriarchal culture, illegal prostitution is a way to control women's sexuality. Men are scared to death to allow women to profit from such a valuable resource. You rarely hear about a high-profile pimp being busted, but it's national news when a madam is arrested!

Having said that, the issue here is not "working girls," but dating women who unknowingly use short-term strategies to attract a long-term relationship.

If, early on, you're allowing him to contribute to your rent, or you're driving his car or accepting valuable gifts, then you're using short-term strategies. If he's only allowed to see you dressed to the nines in the latest fly girl attire, you're using short-term strategies. A new man should also be able to see you on Sunday morning for a run in the park with baggy sweats and no makeup. It tells him you're confident and prepares him for the real you, the one who would be the dominate face in his postbachelor life.

Long-term dating strategies may sound old-fashioned, but they work. Go slow. Don't dress too sexy at the beginning. If you must bare a little skin, choose to expose a little leg, bosom, midriff, or back—but not all four. A plunging neckline and a short skirt are sure signs that you're mostly there for the good times.

Take the time to get to know someone and reveal your true self. After a certain courting period, say five to eight dates, don't limit his sightings of you to good days. Let him see you on other days—sick days, clean-faced, baseball cap days, and bloated PMS days. Don't be afraid to show him you're real. It will make him feel safer about opening up himself.

And for your own good, limit his spending on you to dinner, movies, and tickets. No baubles in the beginning. No jet-set getaways while you're courting. If he pushes, tell him kindly that you feel it's too early, that you don't feel comfortable accepting gifts from someone you don't know well.

I once received a Cartier watch from a man I'd know three weeks. I was so bowled over by his extravagance that I forgot to analyze his motives. This guy was so bad at delaying gratification that he rushed the watch over to me at a doctor's office where he knew I had an appointment. He couldn't even wait until dinner! He also couldn't wait a week before he started courting a second girl on the other coast. Or did she come first? I don't remember. Anyway, what followed for me were seven painful months during which I tried to have a real relationship with a man who obviously thought he'd bought me.

So no gifts at the beginning. A good potential boyfriend will understand. You are trying to make a clear statement that you are a long-term mate, not a professional girlfriend.

Do I Move Too Fast? Despite what God did, your world cannot be created in a week.

Is there any woman on the planet who has not moved too fast in a relationship? It seems to be a curse of our gender, to be leafing through Martha Stewart's wedding issue and perking up our ears at the sound of a De Beers commercial before we've even seen his apartment.

There have been many problems in my own dating history relating to poor choices, but if there is one thing I can take full and complete responsibility for, it is the velocity of my relationships. Ya see, all men want to move at Mach speed—at least toward the bedroom—but we're just as guilty for rushing to get into every other room in the house.

The bottom line: If you want to save your heart, you must learn to pull off of the acceleration and sometimes apply the brakes.

What is an appropriate pace? Here's my expert Wendy opinion of a fairly healthy relationship pace in today's fast world:

1 Don't sleep with him for at least six weeks. In these times of herpes and AIDS, this is an acceptable amount of time. Don't feel pressured by that old third-date rule—that was for the pre-AIDS seventies.

2 Date at least three months before you utter the *boyfriend* word.

3 Date at least a year before you decide to move in.

4 And have conversations about parenting styles, abortion, household finances, and long-term monogamy *before* you buy one wedding magazine.

Am I Willing to Take Emotional Risks? How can we expect intimacy if we don't give it?

What is an emotional risk? Is it revealing on the first date that your heart has been broken three times, that you lost your virginity at fourteen, that you once had an abortion, and that you are an incest survivor? Hell no!

Revealing too many of your deepest feelings and foibles early on is foolish. So, too, is telling a man that you love him, and that your future desire is to have three kids, when you've barely seen six months of couplehood with him. How do you really know for sure if you are in love or just on infatuation's climb up the roller coaster? If it's not possible to be honest with yourself, then you have no business being "honest" with him.

Anyway, none of the things I have mentioned, or ones like them, should be shared until the two of you have established a trusting bond. Then emotional intimacy can begin.

But how do you know when you can trust a man with the secrets of your heart? That's a difficult question that involves a complicated answer.

The question is perhaps better worded: How do you know if you are part of a trusting bond? Well, you will know because you are *part* of that trusting bond. If you question whether a man is trustworthy, then he probably isn't.

Trust is a two-way street and it begins with you. After all, you are not responsible for his behavior. He is. But you are responsible for yours. Being trustworthy yourself means being 100 percent honest about everything. Period. No white lies. No omitted facts. If you're late because you got stuck at the office chatting on iVillage, you can't say your boss made you write a last-minute report. If you cancel on a shared expense date, say a ski weekened, for money reasons, you must also fess up that your financial problem is connected to your trunk full of Nine West boxes. It's all about him getting to know you. And that includes your love of female-bonding chat rooms and trendy shoes.

Honesty also means sometimes saying that you don't yet feel comfortable enough to talk about certain emotional subjects. So your past pains and future fantasies can be your domain until you will it otherwise. That comfort level will come with time, but it is part of a growth process.

Being trustworthy also means being honest with yourself. If you live in a state of denial, believing the external character whom you created is infallible, then you aren't really being honest with yourself or with him. He needs to have tiny peeks into your soul to know that you are human—just like him. He also needs to see a sentry at the gates of your most private thoughts to know that you have boundaries. That will earn you respect.

Knowing when to open up emotionally and how wide to open that door is a matter for your gut, not your head. Of course, if you've had trouble in the past trusting your feelings, or if your "gut" has let you down, you've got to enforce some basic ground rules, so here are some helpful hints:

1 Never, ever lie. Don't try to impress him with any falseness. Don't pretend to make more money than you do, have more suitors than you do, or be busier than you are. Don't "play" hard to get. (Remember, you *are* hard to get!)

2 Decline to answer some questions based on your need for privacy, but make sure you state your clear feelings to him. For instance, if he asks you out for a Monday evening and that is the night you are committed to attend your AA meeting (or whatever), simply say that you have a standing obligation on Monday evenings and it's a personal matter that you hope to share with him someday. Then shut up. If he asks more, simply repeat your statement.

3 Take responsibility for all your choices. Don't blame yourself for your mistakes. Simply acknowledge that any past poor judgments were based on the information and experience that you possessed at the time. If, when these subjects come up, he seems judgmental, don't buy into it. Some food for thought: Negative traits we see in others are those that we often feel about ourselves. If he's judging you, he's probably only questioning his own morals.

4 As a woman you may have to be emotionally vulnerable first. Sorry, it comes with the territory of femaleness. Men need to feel that you've risked something before they do. So carefully choose what you divulge. And yet although you may have to risk first, you don't have to be a martyr.

5 If, after one or two small emotional risks, he's not reciprocating, it's perfectly okay to put the brakes on for a while, or even dump him if your gut tells you to. Opening up more will not entice emotional intimacy. It may just scare him off.

6 If you don't trust him, don't sleep with him. Writer and psychoanalyst Judith Viorst calls it the "riskiest trade of all: sex for love." The odds are definitely not in your favor.

Has Each of My Relationship Choices Gotten Better? We are not lousy girlfriends and do not have failed relationships if we learn and grow from each one.

Look back on all the losers you left or the seemingly great men who got away. Is there a pattern that you recognize? Are there certain "types" that you are a fool for? Are there others that you are finally over? If so, then you have succeeded. You are growing.

I, for one, can safely say that I'm "over" actors and pretty boys. I discovered that an unfair proportion of these cuties have narcissistic tendencies (a need for love that is insatiable) that negate any empathic tools they may possess. In other words, if they require more mirror time than I do, then they probably don't have time to care about my feelings. So in that sense I've evolved and can pat myself on the back.

I've also learned, as I stumble along my cluttered relation-ship path, that I have become a better girlfriend. For instance, I'm now more tolerant of sports addicts since I know that tele-vision sports can be a safe outlet for evolved aggession that is naturally part of a "hunter's" psyche. And, when I see men succeed in business using the principles of teamwork and sportsmanship, I wonder if my anger at sports fans isn't partly jealousy of the important life lessons that come from participating in amateur sports. A couple past boyfriends have taught me that. I'm also better at sharing emotional intimacies. And I'm less inclined to believe that men should think like women. But I know I still have a ways to go.

It wasn't always this way. For a long time both my choices and my reactions to them were constantly repeated. There were a number (don't ask the number!) of men whom I dated who were almost emotional clones of one another. And I became the same feisty and pissed-off bitch with each one! I never thought for a minute that I could have saved myself from their torture by hanging up the phone, walking out of the restaurant, or climbing from their car, and *never looking back.*

In *A Woman's Worth,* the inspirational author and motivational speaker Marianne Williamson tells a great story about recovering from addictions to dangerous men. She says that when a woman is really ill, she doesn't even recognize the snake that is wrapped around her. When her recovery begins, that woman will see a snake, know it is a snake, but still play with it. And yet once she is finally healed, she'll see that snake and cross to the other side of the road.

In *Imperfect Control,* Judith Viorst calls this the knowledge of when to move on. She says it is one of the most crucial of people skills. While it is unhealthy to jump from relationship to relationship, it can be worse to cling to one that is damaging. Like the lyrics in that country and western song, "you have to know when to hold them and when to fold them." Once it's behind you, you can look back and examine it. And remember that you *can* do better next time.

The Boyfriend Test will help you "know when to fold them" so that when it's time to hold one for a long time, he'll hold you back in the same loving way.

Now it is time to turn the page and begin an eye-opening elimination process.

3

designing
a man

> The average woman sees only the
> weak points in a strong man, and
> the good points in a weak one.
> —Elbert Hubbard, *The Note Book*

Did you know that you can have any kind of man in the world? You can have a rich man. You can have a tall man. You can have a powerful man. You can have a family man. You can have a hardworking man. You can have a famous man. You can have a subservient man. You can have a gorgeous man. You can have a health-conscious man.

But—and you knew there would be a but—know that each of these men comes with a unique cocktail of individual life experiences and resulting behavior that may not match your fantasies. Your hardworking man may be a workaholic. Your gorgeous man may be a narcissist. Your family man may be a freeloader. Your health-conscious man may be a control freak. But if that doesn't matter to you (and it should!), I maintain that all these men are attainable.

When I was in college, a girlfriend of mine was reading a most peculiar book. It was called *How to Marry Rich.* In it the author outlined a detailed plan on how any average woman could infiltrate the world of the upper class by appearing at the right schools, country clubs, and resorts, and how she could make herself appealing to a man of "culture." Knowledge of expensive wines, watches, and other pricey whims helps. And since wealthy men tend to have a wider range of women to choose from and the competition is steep, this book even gave fashion tips. What fashion won't erase, it advised, a little plastic surgery might. Even an ugly duckling (is there really such a thing in the female race?) can transform herself to be appealing to her Dream Man, if nabbing him is *that* important to her.

Years later I sat in a restaurant in Aspen and listened while a twenty-four-year-old Iowa farm girl, now a bleached blonde with a perfect nose job, held a certain collection of men enraptured with her banter about the merits of purchasing a G-4 over a G-3 (for us average folks, she was referring to models of private jets). I found her conversation to be comical. This young girl could no more afford a jet than the men at the table could, though they were still wealthy by most people's standards. To me this girl looked silly—a fraud. To the men, however, she looked like a prize, a woman whose knowledge obviously came from the circles she traveled in—perhaps from pillow talk with their competition. They lapped up her conversation like a bunch of nerdy schoolboys vying for the quarterback's girlfriend. It was then that I realized that this woman was very smart. Smart enough to go for what she wanted, that is, even if her desires were questionable.

And if it could be done to obtain a rich man, then it could be done to attract a tall man, a smart man, a mogul, a kid-loving man, a mechanic, a martial artist, a macho-man, a military man, a mailman, or a millinery expert. In short, "it" could be done to catch anyone.

But "it" means transforming yourself into the desires of another. "It" means suppressing your deepest needs to entice a man. "It" means denying a part of yourself. "It" often means submitting to the control of others, or at least to their tastes at the expense of your own. And "it" may not be worth it.

I know from whence I speak. I used to be the queen of those transformations. My weak boundaries were chipped away during childhood as my likes and dislikes were dictated by my parents, rather than by my own predilections. The result: I became quick to sense the pleasures, needs, and desires of others. Fearing, as all children do, some kind of abandonment, I became the ultimate people-pleaser to my parents—and later, to everyone else. I became a chameleon, subtly altering my dress, my semantics, my vocal tone, even my morals, to accommodate the desires of a friend, a boss, or the man in front of me. The man who would somehow complete me.

I could entice him, but I soon learned that I really didn't want to live with him forever.

That's the caveat. You can attract any man you think you want, but are you really ready to acquire all the baggage that goes along with him? Do you really want the ambitious man who puts work above family, the family man who doesn't put effort into a romantic relationship with you, the tall, gorgeous man who isn't much more than that, the famous man who loves himself more than you, or the health-conscious man who denies you the odd piece of beef? I realize that I'm talking in clichés here, but stereotypes run rampant in our culture because they often contain some kernel of truth, PC or not.

Remember the Sunday-school adage: Be careful what you pray for because you might get it.

Having just said that, I feel a need to add that I believe that women of weak boundaries (remember, fully one-third of us) don't really know what they dislike until they have it. Having our infantile needs finally met as an adult with a conscious mind is an eye-opener. Your dreams may become your nightmares now that you have a mature, individualized perspective. The child in you screams, "I want him! I want him!" And the adult in you silently watches until it's time to say, "Yuck!"

Thus the perpetual mating game. As I've said before, the point of the Boyfriend Test is to reduce the number of roller-coaster plunges in your love life, but if there is some aspect of a man—his money, his car, his penis size—that appeals to you as a "must-have," then you may have to get it to realize that you don't really need it after all.

So look not with an air of disdain over the superficial nature of some of the categories in the upcoming boyfriend candidate profile. Yes, you may ask for a certain look, a certain income, and even a certain car. It's your choice. There are some women reading this who must have a man with a G-3 in which to fly far away from their Iowa farm. Of course, the farther they get, the more homesick they may become. It's all a matter of perspective.

Men Are Like Pizza

Creating the man for you can be as easy as buying a new car or having a pizza delivered to your door. That idea may sound a little crazy, but it's not as far-fetched as you might think.

Take my example of a pizza delivery. Step 1: Your stomach starts to growl, signaling to your brain that you have a desire. Step 2: You take action by picking up the phone. As you place your order, you remember which toppings you liked in the past, say, tomatoes, olives, and hot peppers, and forgo those you definitely hated, like anchovies. Step 3: You set your table and wait about thirty minutes to welcome a hot Italian with no fishy aftertaste.

The same formula can be used when selecting a man. Step 1: You know you're ready to meet a man when you've passed the Girlfriend Test and your brain has suppressed all fond memories of a single life, temporarily replacing them with visions of domestic bliss. (Don't worry, you'll remember some great things about being single once you're married, but that's for another book.)

Step 2: You take action by picking up a pen. As you begin

to place an order for a man, you remember all the toppings you liked in the past and forgo those you didn't. You can take the cute smile from one and the tight butt from another. You can ignore one's cheap-skate spending habits and highlight his punctuality. In this first "order," write down everything you liked about your past boyfriends, followed by everything you hated about them. (My chart on page 82 will help you.) Imagine that you are creating a girlfriend's version of a police composite drawing.

When you're done drawing up your list, review it carefully. Then put it in a drawer for a day or two and come back to it often, crossing out what's superfluous and adding forgotten important features.

Step 3: You set your table and wait. When your list is finally completed, paste it into your dream journal or scrapbook for future reference, and then send a clear message out to the universe that this man is your intention. Last, get busy with putting your house in order.

"The universe?" you ask. Okay, I know you think that I'm nuts, or its equivalent; that I'm a Californian. But I promise, I wouldn't go spacey with the "universe" references if it hadn't worked for me.

"Sending a message to the universe" is really just an adjustment in your perception. For you to meet an appropriate man, you must first really believe that he exists and that you really deserve him. Once that is clear in your head, you'll be unconsciously inviting him in by ignoring all mismatches. Heck, even your body language will change, sending a signal about your desires.

Still skeptical? Think back to the first time you bought a car. You were quite pleased with yourself that you had finally attained the fiscal strength to save a down payment and be eligible for a bank loan or lease. Read: You passed the Girlfriend Test. Then you combed the classifieds, talked to friends and family about makes and models, and thought about all the nice cars that you had been in in the past. Finally you decided on the exact make, model, year, and color that would suit you perfectly. Read: You designed your man.

I bet in the few weeks before your car arrived, you tended to spot it in traffic, on TV, in magazines. Suddenly you noticed your intended car everywhere! This vehicle that seemed only a dream the year before had become virtually ubiquitous and was finally attainable. And the same thing works with a man.

If He's the "One" for You, He's Too Good to Be True

The first technique to designing a man is to throw out the notion that there is "one" man for you. It's an archaic concept sold by an old culture that wanted to add a romantic hue to lifelong monogamy. In days of old, women were supposed to be happy if they found the "one" and stayed with him forever. But finding the "one" is an illusion, and if we cling to such an illusion, we can mistakenly confuse short-term attraction with deep, committed love.

A note about short-term attraction: It feels like the heated romantic love of a Harlequin romance or Hollywood movie. From Cinderella to *Pretty Woman,* our culture is filled with mythology designed to convince women that a single man can solve their problems. Short-term attraction has your adrenaline charging, your sexuality in high gear—and your brain in neutral. Unfortunately, it most often ends as quickly as it begins. And in their disappointment, women who buy into this notion of a "one and only" continue in a futile search.

Deep, committed love, on the other hand, feels more like a friendship than a fling. It takes time to evolve and eventually has a comfort level as cozy as an old cashmere sweater.

This does not mean that there are only two kinds of love and never the twain shall meet. Deep, committed love often starts out as a short-term attraction that, if paced properly and not sabotaged by one's childhood issues, grows into the other kind. In this millennium there are plenty of "ones" who have the potential to commit to deeper intimacy.

And if you've played your cards right by dealing with your own issues first and then attempting to have a relationship based on more than superficial attraction, you can begin to break out of your cycle of going from heartbreak to heartbreak.

I've already said that long-term commitment should be the goal, but sometimes, even with all our best efforts, it doesn't work out. The difference between those types of breakups and the roller-coaster ride of going from "big crush" to "bigger crush" is that you learn something about yourself after a valiant effort in choosing better and being a better girlfriend. Next time won't be a repeat, it'll be a graduation to a new level of relationship.

However, there's one more caveat to feeling good about serial monogamy. Even though serial monogamy is the way of life in America and is often an advancement from the long-term hellish marriages of the past, we shouldn't consider leaving a man just because we've had a bad week, month, or sometimes year. A relationship should end when all the lessons have been learned on both sides of the union.

The reality is that a healthy relationship is filled with change and personal growth. And the challenge for both people is to change individually while accommodating each other's changes. A relationship is a constant reshaping of boundaries. On the one hand it is a war over personal freedom, and on the other a clinging desire for closeness. It is the ultimate tug-of-war.

Sometimes the rope breaks under the stress. One partner surges ahead in growth and leaves the other behind. Or both partners become numb to each other's needs, or their own! This is how relationships end.

When a fickle girlfriend decides to trade her man in for an older or richer or better-looking boyfriend, she isn't growing. When she trades him in for a smarter or kinder man, she is.

Be Realistic in Your Creation

If you've never created a projected boyfriend profile or have been unsuccessful with similar lists in the past, allow me to offer some helpful girlfriend tips.

First, don't make the list too long. If you're looking for a man with twenty-seven perfect personality and physical features, you're coming dangerously close to looking for the "one." And, as I've said, he doesn't exist.

Likewise, if your list includes exotic or unique characteristics, you might be hard up to find a match. Ditto on highly unlikely combinations: There are few athletes, actors, or rock stars who read the classics and prefer quiet nights at home in blissful monogamy to nights on the town. Sound clichéd? Yep, but as I said, at the risk of sounding very un-PC, I maintain that all stereotypes are based on some truth that long ago started the domino effect of bad publicity. Are there exceptions to these stereotypes? Of course there are. And for heaven's sake, if you meet one, snap him up! Are there many? I don't believe so. And if you're over thirty, you probably don't want to play a low-odds game.

I have a *very* smart guy friend. He's highly educated, well read, funny, and emotionally aware. His problem is he's looking for the same combination in a woman—with supermodel good looks. I keep telling him that, despite the many women who have the potential to grow into such well-rounded and downright powerful creatures, our culture produces few. From the get-go, beautiful girls in our society tend to be steered away from science, politics, or the social sciences and directed toward the arts—or worse, beauty pageants and European runways.

When I was modeling as a teen in Paris, I found that my path in life at that point resembled that of a male athlete—my teachers let me off class for big auditions not unlike a football player for college tryouts. The message was clear: Your potential to be a success in our society (namely make big money) is best weighted with your physical attributes. College was promoted to me as a four-year rite of passage rather than a route to professional advancement.

There are still far fewer women in medical school and law school than there are men. And despite the job opportunities spawned by the technological revolution, the number of women studying computer science has been on the decline since it peaked in the mideighties. Now, how many of those women look like Cindy or Claudia? I'm not saying that all the models in the world couldn't be NASA scientists, anthropologists, or biologists. I'm saying that it would be a hard battle for them to pursue their intellectual dreams, given the bias—and pressures—in our culture to do otherwise.

So my friend who would love to be discussing Proust, or debating social issues, finds himself at parties with models who talk about Prada, D&G, and jet lag. He's forty-two years old and waiting to find the exception to the stereotype. (Or is he protecting himself from a real relationship?) I think he should edit his search criteria.

As for *your* search criteria, there are few men who possess leading-man good looks, concern for the environment, intellectual prowess, humor, and a Bill Gates bank account! So be real, girls.

Rich Is Not Necessarily Better

We would all like to hook up with a man with funds, right? If you said no, then you are denying yourself one of your most primitive desires. (By the way, Denial stands for "Don't Even Notice I Am Lying.")

As I mentioned in the Girlfriend Test in Chapter 2, we are all anthropologically designed to get excited over a man with resources. Our cavewomen ancestors who carried that trait found more food on the table and more clothes on the backs of their babies. Thus, their offspring were more likely to survive and reproduce, and inherit their mothers' taste for furs.

Those women who were attracted to men for, say, their sense of humor probably begot hungry babes who laughed a lot but may not have lived to reproduce. In the end, we evolved into a population of women whose deepest animal instinct is to foster the survival of our offspring. And to do that, we needed the protection and resources of a man.

However, as I mentioned in Chapter 1, "Welcome to the Girls' Club," we are at an evolutionary crossroads: Most women today are also economically independent, yet we still carry that old gene that jumps for joy when a limo shows up to take us to dinner.

Our offspring, however, do not need Cartier watches to survive. Nor do we. The next question we should ask ourselves is: Is our desire to date a wealthy man designed to benefit our offspring or ourselves? And why would *we* need such benefits?

This is one of those areas where psychology and anthropology overlap. Yes, we all have inherited a desire for men with resources. But only people with certain damage to their confidence, in *this* lifetime, "need" to be wealthy beyond their requirements for warmth, food, and shelter, and good schools. Maybe they need to be liked. They need to be loved. Just make sure you aren't playing into these needs.

I used to be one who thought rich was better. (How brazenly I use the past tense here!) I dated some wealthy men and it was those experiences that showed me how people use money as a crutch. As the arm piece of a few rich men, I became a voyeur into the world of the wealthy and found a petri dish ripe for a personality study.

I found that cocktail parties and formal dinners, unlike what you see in glamorous James Bond movies, were mostly sandboxes for kids to brag about their toys. If these adults weren't bragging about their toys, they were inquiring of one another which toy they were "supposed to be" buying next. And if they couldn't acquire a certain toy, they criticized it—like a frustrated child screaming, "I don't want it, anyway!"

As a news reporter, I once sat in the back of a luxurious helicopter with a certain (in)famous real-estate tycoon. He was remarking that he had seen me the night before interviewing supermodel Claudia Schiffer. Then, unprompted by me, he began to critique her body, telling me her thighs were too fat and her hips too wide. I remind you, he was talking about one of the most beautiful female specimens to ever grace the planet! What does that say about him? Had he hit on her once and been rejected? Perhaps he was really screaming, "I don't want her, anyway!"

All this is to say that the haystack gets higher if you limit your search for a good man to a rich man. Not that there aren't smart, witty, worldly, conscious men out there who live in big mansions, but they're probably already married to their college sweethearts.

A Note About the Chart

On the next few pages, you will find a chart to help you design your man. Read through the chart carefully and circle all the characteristics that appeal to you. There is no limit on selections on your first pass. In some categories you might circle one trait. In others there may be many things that appeal to you. There are also spaces to add your own ideas and descriptions.

Initially, don't be concerned if your list is too long and detailed. Later I'll give you a formula to pare it down to something more reasonable. For instance, if you're an equal-opportunity dater, you may find that you've circled all ethnic categories. In your final chart, race won't appear, because it doesn't narrow down your choices. It shows how open you are to any right man.

So get your pencil in hand. It's time to create your man.

THE

boyfriend

TEST

CANDIDATE PROFILE

_me_   age 14   √ = choice

1. Looks

Height _____

Hair ~~Blondy~~ Brown / Blond   Brown

Eyes dk Brown   Brown

Body Type _____

2. Age

☐ 18–25

☐ 26–35

☐ 36–45

☐ 46–60

☐ 61–100

3. Education

- ☐ High School
- ☐ Some College or other Specialty School
- ☐ Completed a University Degree
- ☐ Master's Degree
- ☐ Ph.D.

4. Wardrobe

- ☐ Business
- ☐ Grunge
- ☐ Academic
- ☐ Athletic
- ☐ High Fashion
- ☐ Gap/Banana Republic
- ☑ Other _baseball t's_

5. Ethnicity

- ☐ Asian/Pacific Islander
- ☐ Black
- ☐ Biracial
- ☑ Caucasian
- ☐ Euro-Boy
- ☐ Hispanic
- ☐ Middle Easterner
- ☐ Other _____

6. Religion

- ☐ Agnostic
- ☐ Atheist
- ☐ Buddhist
- ☐ Christian
- ☐ Fanatical Cult
- ☐ Hindu
- ☐ Jewish ☑ none
- ☐ Muslim
- ☐ New Age

7. Personality

- ☐ Introvert
- ☐ Extrovert
- ☑ Comedian
- ☑ Thinker
- ☑ Philosopher
- ☐ Caregiver
- ☐ Ruler
- ☐ Innocent
- ☐ Warrior

8. Relationship History

- ☐ Divorced
- ☑ Single
- ☐ Been Engaged
- ☐ Children...etc.

9. Family

- ☑ Came from Two-Parent Household
- ☐ Raised Primarily by Mother
- ☐ Raised Primarily by Father
- ☐ Raised by Relatives
- ☐ Raised by MTV
- ☐ Raised by Wolves (just kidding)
- ☐ Many Siblings
- ☑ Few Siblings
- ☐ Only Child
- ☐ Cloned in a Lab

10. Politics

- ☐ Conservative
- ☐ Liberal
- ☐ Reform
- ☐ Radical Anarchist

11. Home

- ☑ Apartment
- ☑ Townhouse
- ☑ Single-Family Home
- ☑ Modern
- ☑ Traditional
- ☐ Lives with Roommates
- ☐ Lives with Mom and Dad

12 Pets

- [ ] Dog Person
- [x] Cat Person
- [ ] Horse Person
- [ ] Fish Person
- [ ] Bird Person
- [ ] Person Person

13. Wheels

- [ ] Environmentally Friendly
- [ ] SUV
- [ ] Sedan
- [ ] Sports Car
- [ ] Pickup Truck
- [ ] Luxury Car
- [ ] Motorcycle
- [ ] Bicycle
- [ ] Public Transit
- [ ] Feet

14. Career

- [ ] Relatively Stable
- [ ] Freelance
- [ ] Creative/Artistic
- [ ] Works with Hands
- [ ] Performer
- [ ] Management Type

☑ Professional (Doctor, Lawyer, Accountant)
☑ Analytical/Mathematical
☐ Entrepreneurial
☑ Caregiver/Social Worker

15. Income

Minimum Salary _____
Maximum Salary _____

16. Schedule

☑ Day Worker
☐ Night Worker
☐ Long Hours
☐ Short Hours
☐ Flexible Schedule
☐ Works Weekends
☐ Works Various Shifts
☐ Travels for Business
☐ Stays in One City

17. Leisure Time

List your two favorite leisure activities that you'd
prefer to do with a man—i.e., rollerblading, skiing,
antiquing, stamp collecting, theater, museums,
golfing, etc.

1. _watching TV & cuddling_
2. _eating out_
   Sports, games

CARDS

18. Music

- ☑ Rock
- ☐ R&B
- ☐ Alternative
- ☐ Jazz
- ☐ Country
- ☑ Classical
- ☐ Opera
- ☐ Pop
- ☐ World Beat

19. Film

- ☑ Action
- ☑ Comedy
- ☑ Drama
- ☐ Art House
- ☐ Foreign Language

20. Television

- ☑ Sitcoms
- ☐ News
- ☑ Movies
- ☑ Sports
- ☐ Magazine Shows
- ☑ Cable (Discovery, A&E, History Channels)

21. Exercise

- ☐ Trains Competitively
- ☐ Three-to-Five-Times-a-Week Gym Rat
- ☐ Weekend Warrior
- ☐ Outdoor Sports Only
- ☐ Moderate (Walks/Cycles Only)
- ☐ Couch Potato

6

22. Diet

- ☑ Carnivore
- ☐ Low-Fat Varied Diet
- ☐ Fish-Eating Vegetarian
- ☐ Egg and Dairy Vegetarian
- ☐ Vegan

5

23. Drugs

How much can you tolerate him using?

Caffeine ___Sure, if he wants___

Alcohol ___Not often___

Tobacco ___None___

Marijuana ___None___

Other Drugs ___None___

What About Smart and Nice?

Did you notice that my chart has two glaring omissions? I hope by now you are screaming, "This woman is so superficial! What about *kindness?* What about *intelligence?*"

Kindness and intelligence are the two most crucial characteristics of a romantic partner. And if you've dealt with your own issues outlined in the Girlfriend Test, thankfully, you'll unconsciously choose these traits in a man with or without my direction.

Our sexual psychology was once dissected by renowned evolutionary psychologist David Buss. In a huge study of more than ten thousand men and women from cultures around the world, subjects were asked to rank dozens of physical and psychological characteristics they looked for in perspective mates. The results were the same all over the planet: The characteristics judged most important in a mate, whether male or female, were kindness and intelligence. The fact that both genders chose these traits as important is not startling—both are crucial for engaging in the complex give-and-take needed in any intimate relationship, especially one that involves the considerable responsibility of bringing up well-adjusted children.

And the third most important trait? Well, that's where the genders differed. Men said they sought youth and beauty in women and women sought resources in men. Obviously these traits are still existent in cultures around the world, but the best news for any woman should be that our age and looks aren't the most important thing to most men. They came in third!

The only women who should be concerned about not finding kindness and intelligence in a mate are those who don't recognize it easily. These are women whose perception of kindness is a bit askew. If you are unsure about your definition of kindness, the Boyfriend Test will help you become more clear, but it is your duty to your soul to work on all your own issues before judging men.

Make Your List Manageable

Now it's time to narrow down your choices to create a realistic picture of your future boyfriend.

I urge you to take some time with your list. This is your creation. God didn't make the earth in one day. She took an entire week. Pray on this. Meditate on it. Get drunk and talk about it. Ask both your exterior self and your interior soul what you really want. And don't be afraid to be honest with your ego. Your future depends on it.

While you are doing all this soul-searching, begin to cross off items that are not so important to you, and put stars beside ones that are crucial to your current definition of happiness.

Now I want you to reduce your list to ten characteristics. Did you hear me? *Ten.* No more. No less. Here are some helpful ways to do this:

✔ First look for obvious contradictions. If he's an introvert, how can he also be a performer? If he smokes cigarettes, there's little chance that he's an athletic vegetarian. If he hates organized religion, then he probably won't be voting Republican. Examine your contradictions and make a choice of one over the other.

✔ If you circled many answers in one category, then eliminate the category entirely. Obviously you're ambivalent about it, so it may not be a deal-breaker in dating negotiations.

✔ Finally, if your list contains one extreme, picky stickler of an item, ask yourself if you've left it there as a land mine. For example, if your favorite movie was *Gone With the Wind* and his was *Con Air,* are you really going to kick him out of bed? Or are you just looking for an excuse to dump him?

I can't stress enough how much time you have to take with this list. Defining your man by only ten criteria is a difficult task. And the next part of the Boyfriend Test asks that you stick with this list for some time, so be sure about it.

When it is finally complete, print it out in boldface. Tape it to your refrigerator. Put it under your pillow. Read it over twice a day. Know this list inside and out, for these criteria will be your ten commandments for your next roller-coaster ride in Relationship Park.

Now here are the two most important rules for success with the Boyfriend Test.

1 Do not go out with *anyone* who shows wild divergence from this list during the initial Meet and Greet and the Telephone Test.

2 Do not alter your list until you have dated three men who seem to fit this profile. After that, you might consider altering it *only slightly* to invite in a wider range of candidates. But don't open the barn door, or the stampede of unlikely candidates might trample down your boundaries.

Now proceed, my girlfriends. The amusement park awaits you.

TEST
him

a t this point, all of your internal work should be under way. I might add that looking inside ourselves is an ongoing life project. Don't stop improving yourself once you're snuggled up with a boyfriend. That's when the real work of personal growth begins because you will then have a sounding board, a cheerleader, and an adversary. And your reactions to all of his behavior can be quite enlightening.

But before you get there, you have to choose wisely. Sometimes that means you have to reject a relationship that feels comfortable though not stimulating. Or it may mean you must remain part of a relationship that's a bit irritating because it may be the one that teaches you the most about yourself—especially if you can't get away with your usual bad behavior.

And, don't lose sight of the fact that you are not the same woman who entered relationships in the past. You are conscious. You are growing. You are a catch, girlfriend.

the meet and greet

> Gretel looked at him and blinked. She wondered if she had grown extremely stupid. Why was it that she trusted what he was saying?
> —Alice Hoffman, *Local Girls*

So you wanna meet a wonderful man. Good. That means you're probably a living, breathing heterosexual woman, who's in tune with her biological urges, and intent on having an evolved relationship. Here's good news: He does exist. Here's the bad news: He's hidden under a haystack of penile infantiles. Translation: The world is filled with men whose biological desire to have a relationship far outweighs their emotional ability to have one.

Of course, all men are not pigs. Most men, God willing,

will eventually, at some point during their life span, have a dedicated, loving, evolved relationship. But most men within your sight line today probably aren't ready. Thus the daunting haystack.

Step One: Fire the Low-Performance Boyfriend

Take it from the world-weary girls' club. It's not worth waiting for a dysfunctional man to achieve dramatic personal growth. Even if your patience and eggs endure, his ability to see you as partner material will wane with his growth. It's Murphy's Law. He'll eventually grow to despise the old him and anything that went along with it. Remember, the first woman who supported him while he grew up was rewarded with an empty nest and laundry duty on weekends.

One television producer friend of mine fell in "love" with a great man while shooting a show in France. When she returned to Los Angeles, what followed were two years of long letters, high phone bills, and no-shows at LAX. She kept believing that this man was going to follow his word rather than his actions and show up in America one day to sweep her off her feet. For two years she dated no one except this Dream Man in her head who remained an ocean away. All the while he led her along, his letters riddled with "I love you's" and fantasies about their future together in the United States. Believe it or not, the final straw came only when she learned that he had, in fact, visited the U.S. a number of times during their imaginary relationship. Once he even got as close to her as San Francisco. Yet he never visited her once!

If only my friend had subjected him to the Boyfriend Test and been strong enough to fail him, she would have saved herself a lot of time and heartache. The process of finding a great man is really one of discarding a great many men. It may take some time, so be prepared for a long search.

Step Two: Test Him on First Meeting

If you spent time pondering the questions in the Girl-friend Test and completed the chart in Chapter 3, you now have a clear idea of who you are and what exactly you're looking for. Now it's time to go on the offense and separate the wheat from the chaff.

Your first opportunity comes when you first set eyes on a potential boyfriend candidate. That first look-see is the most important time to have all your wits about you. Forget everything you've heard about Cupid and the cosmos coming together. Your protective radar should be fully operative at this moment and enable you to spot a bad boyfriend. This is especially important if he's tall and gorgeous.

It's amazing how much you can tell about someone in just a few minutes of conversation—that is, if you can reduce the volume on your pounding heart. With any luck, a loser will reveal himself right away and you can make your escape long before you give up your phone number.

First and foremost, whether in bars or restaurants, at sporting events or malls, or on the street, a good boyfriend candidate never approaches a woman without an invitation to do so. Any man who doesn't at least get our attention before he moves into our personal space is making a social blunder. Our primate ancestors had no information on whether or not an approaching male was a suitor or a rapist unless he exhibited social graces. His highly evolved social graces *should* invite a beckon from you, if you so desire.

Your invitation can be issued in many forms. It's something you've probably been doing all along but haven't been aware of it. The most common are the age-old hair flip and the quick glance at him followed by eyes that dart downward when he tries to meet yours. A simple smile is a sure thing. Open body language with an exposed neck is something sex researchers also say is a shoo-in.

Are your arms folded across your chest? Is your head down? Are your shoulders slumped? You could be sending an unconscious rebuff.

Are you running your fingers through your hair? Are you sitting up on your tailbone? How about licking your lips? All are signs, according to researchers who study body language, of a woman ready to greet a man.

Where to Scout for Boyfriend Candidates

Meeting a man is like being a great headhunter who scouts for talent. If you want to draft a star to a team, be prepared to scout all the college campuses and small companies.

You probably already know the good traditional meeting spots: health clubs, malls, restaurants, bars, and sporting events. Well, welcome to the new millennium. Here are the newest spots: industry trade shows (work those booths, especially if you're in a cool industry!), the Internet, Starbucks (bring a laptop and work on a screenplay or novel). And don't rule out airplanes, church, and traffic jams.

I know one couple who met at a funeral! The mother of their mutual friend had passed away, and Cupid swooped down in the parking lot while the two were waiting to leave. Both said they felt very funny flirting at a funeral, but a few weeks later, when their mutual friend's grieving had begun to subside, that guy got the gumption to call and inquire about being set up with his parking-lot heartthrob.

QUESTION #1

Does He Approach Without an Invitation? If a guy is in your face too quickly, he's a reject. This kind of strong

advance makes us question his motives or at least his social skills.

Of course, a good boyfriend candidate knows that if he doesn't get an invitation right away, he can cautiously try to solicit one. The first step to soliciting an invitation is to make sure he's in your sight line. A confident man might consider the possibility that you're not wearing your contact lenses and missed his room-stopping good looks, so he'll take the long route to the men's room if it passes by your table. If that's not working, he'll give you that determined guy-glance. You know the one. No, not the up-and-down "What's at the top of those legs?" look, but rather the cool guy, "I'm a little interested in what I see" look.

At that point he should have entered your consciousness. If he's got a chance with you, this is the time to issue the invitation. However, even nice guys sometimes miss signals. He could be mistaking your hair flip for a hair-teasing technique. If he really wants to get a polite confirmation that it's okay to approach you, he might pass by one more time and utter one simple word: "Hi." That's it. No more. No less. If he says more, he's working too fast.

It's your job now to catch the pitch. If you're interested, respond. If you're not, don't. Or, if you're a believer in Dear Abby's dictum that a response to a greeting is good manners, you might return with a bitchy-girl "Hello." You know the one. That's when you have a tone of voice that says, "Who are you to be entering my realm?" If you project just the right disinterested, greater-than-thou inflection, he'd be an idiot to pursue further.

It's true that the world's most powerful aphrodisiac is the word *no,* so be clear, firm, but polite...or you'll never get rid of him. I know one girl who is afraid to be honest this way, so she's sweet to every guy she meets. Consequently every guy she meets thinks he has a chance with her. In the end she spends most of her time hiding behind her answering machine. At one point I got her to admit that this litany of man-messages is really just an ego booster for her. She confided to me that her deepest fear is that if she alters her behavior, no man will ever call again. This couldn't be further from the truth. True, fewer inappropriate men will call, but I promise, a good boyfriend will. Right now, if her Dream Man is watching from afar, he can assume that she's simply a player-chick and not interested in a serious relationship.

Remember that the art of finding a good boyfriend is about eliminating the losers early on. And you must be strong about it. As the Nike ads say, "Just Do It!" And remember that strength is as attractive in women as it is in men.

QUESTION #2

Does He Refer to Women As Girls? Unless he dates someone under the age of eighteen, which isn't legal unless he was

born in the eighties himself, we are not girls!

Exception: He can use the term *girlfriend* when talking about past or future relationships. This implies monogamy. This is good.

Here's an easy first-round elimination tip that will save you from going on a useless date. He's probably not a great guy if his language is immature.

To each other, of course we are girlfriends. We belong to the girls' club and we attend girls' night out. But to men we are women. Period.

A lesson in semantics: After feeling the wrath of a woman misnamed, one man innocently mused to me that he always thought the noun *girl* is the opposite of *guy*, a relatively innocuous term. In fact, *girl* is the opposite of *boy*, and implies youth, inexperience, and powerlessness, as in ball boy. At this point in the English language there is no feminine term that bridges the time of life between girl and woman like *guy* does for boy and man. So if a man attempting to create a favorable first impression misuses this term, he is at the very least uninformed. There's also a good chance he's an insecure guy who uses the term in a condescending way to boost his own self-esteem. He could be frightened of a fully evolved female. Not a good sign. You need a confident man. If happiness is carried in your baggage, confidence should be neatly tucked away in his.

Is His Focus Your Body Over Your Brain? True, guys notice a woman's physical attributes first, but if he can't get past it in his initial conversation and too much attention is placed on your beauty, walk away.

Yes, we know it's flattering. We love it when they compliment us. And we love to turn guys on. But you can assume that if he has approached you, he *is* turned on. To say it out loud, and in many ways, even through jokes, means that turned on is *all* he is.

One girlfriend of mine recently met a man who spent most of their conversation telling her how beautiful she is. She recounted their conversation to me over a manicure the next day. "My hair really didn't look *that* great. My makeup wasn't *that* beautiful, and I'm not in the best shape of my life, but if you were eavesdropping on our conversation, you'd think the guy was talking to Tyra Banks! It made him seem completely insincere."

Granted, your Dream Man wants your body. But he also wants your head and your heart and your soul, not necessarily in that order.

A savvy Dream Man will have balance in his first conversation with you. He may ask about your job, your hobbies, your family, etc. He'll tell you about himself. He may even slip in one polite comment about how attractive you are, but he won't dwell there. He's too cool and smart for that. Beware of the man who keeps bringing the conversation back to compliments about your physical features. He brings it back to your looks 'cause he's looking to bring you home...and probably not for an extended stay.

Does He Disrespect Relationship Boundaries? If you have a boyfriend or he has a girlfriend and this guy is hitting on you, disqualify him fast. You know the old adage: If he's doing it to her, he'll do it to you.

This especially applies if either of you is married. It's your obligation as a card-carrying member of the girls' club to police your man. And don't fall for any of that "She doesn't understand me, you're my true love" crap! I've been there. I've heard it all. If he respects you and he respects himself, he'll make himself a single man *before* he approaches you.

And make sure he really is single when he says so. Some men can be sneaky. One girlfriend I know (who shall remain nameless, though her initials are W.W.) had been politely refusing the advances of a married man but was encouraged when he finally told her he had left his wife. She decided then to break down and go on a date with him. Afterward he took her to his "new" apartment, and within a week he had her in the sack. By week two he was back with his wife. In truth the guy whose apartment he was borrowing came back into town. The lecherous married man had never left his wife in the first place.

On the other hand, if he's single and you're the one with a boyfriend or husband, any guy hitting on you is a complete loser. Not only does he disrespect the girls' club, he's ignoring the boys' club. And that can be downright dangerous! With-hold your phone number.

QUESTION #5

Does He Ignore Workplace Boundaries? The game of love can be played almost anywhere. It is not illegal to approach you in any public place. However, if he's been following the advancement of sexual harass-ment prosecution, he's clueless if he approaches you at the office.

First of all, if he's your superior, he's breaking the law. Politely tell him so and document any negative changes in his behavior after the rebuff.

If he's an underling, and you date him, *your* career could be on the line. Imagine that this workplace romance doesn't take off. Then six months after what you thought was a cordial breakup he gets fired for an unrelated reason. He now has a great case to sue *you* for sexual harassment. He can claim that because he broke up with you, you made his life miserable at work and eventually got him fired. Cases have been won on this basis.

Most companies today have policies prohibiting romantic relationships between employees. Although it seems like it would be safe to date someone on the same level, in fact, labor attornies discourage it on every level. My advice: Respect this boundary. Put romantic blinders on at work. Find a boyfriend at the gym.

Did I mention traffic jams? Sometimes they can be an unusual but opportune place to meet someone. I know a woman who met her true love in a traffic jam. Well, actually, she met her true love's slimy best friend, but this led to meeting her man. This guy, the creep, kept hailing her at red lights because he spotted her out-of-state license plates. Or maybe he just smelled fresh meat in town. In any case, at each light, he kept dropping names of people he knew in her home state through his open window until, miracle of all miracles, he hit on a name she recognized. Next, he begged her to pull over for two minutes so he could call the mutual acquaintance. Since it was a busy street in broad daylight, she took the risk. Once on the phone, that woman back home, forgetting for a moment her girls' club loyalty, gave a glowing report on the traffic-jam gigolo but neglected to mention that he was married!

A week later she naively goes out to lunch with the trying-to-cheat hubby and they happen to run into his single and, thankfully, ethical friend. The good catch of a guy, knowing the habits of his unscrupulous friend, sizes up the situation in a heartbeat. That afternoon, he calls the philanderer, lays a serious guilt trip on him, and demands the woman's phone number. Voilà! She gets a call from her Dream Man. Of course, this whole scenario could have backfired. The Dream Man could have seen her as his buddy's mistress and disqualified her. Luckily for her, he preferred to see a damsel in distress.

It makes sense that you should scout for men in places that you like to go. There you will find compatible men who share your interests. If you're a devoted basketball fan, then look for him in the stands, at the concession booth, or in the traffic jam on the way out. If you love to read, and picture long Sunday mornings lying in bed with magazines and a warm, hard body, then try a bookstore.

Having said that, though, there is also something to be said for breaking out of your mold and expanding your world. Good headhunters don't limit themselves to their hometowns in search of prize candidates. Nor should you limit yourself to your small world when looking for a boyfriend. When we go through our days in a routine manner, walking or driving the same route, using the same dry cleaners, working out at the same health club, life becomes automatic and we end up wearing blinders. Somehow, when our surroundings are familiar, we don't notice anything around us. That's a problem when you could be surrounded by wonderful men at this very moment.

One girlfriend of mine, a successful advertising sales rep,

says she never meets men when she's in her home city, but whenever she's on a business trip, attractive men seem to pop up everywhere. Her plight is understandable. It's because in unfamiliar surroundings our eyes are wide open. We're alert, scanning for street signs, hailing cabs, looking for ATMs, a piece of pizza, or a nail salon…and suddenly our guy-radar is fully functioning. I think that's why so many of my gal pals are in long-distance relationships. (An expensive relationship option, by the way.)

So if you want to meet someone close to home, if you feel you're in a rut and haven't met anyone new for a while, change your routine. You might be pleasantly surprised at what suddenly appears in your line of vision.

Also, if you hang out with the girls a lot, steer them to some guy-friendly locales. One night I took a single girlfriend to a hockey game and I thought her neck was going to break. She was so used to hanging with the girls, grabbing a salad and a tearjerker movie, that it was as if I'd landed her on Planet Man.

Think about where men hang out alone or in packs. A sports bar on fight night. Ski hills. Gyms. Home Depot. Auto-body shops. (Put some lipstick on next time you take your car in.) And yes, driving ranges.

HOW TO EXPAND
Your Vision on Your Home-Turf Hunting Ground

1 Try a new breakfast spot.

2 Move to a different StairMaster.

3 Switch dry cleaners.

4 Sign up for a night course.

5 Shop at a new market.

6 Vacation at a mountain rather than a beach. (Guys take girls to the tropics and join other guys at ski hills.)

7 Do something culturally in your own city that you've never done before: a museum, a play, a symphony.

8 Try a new car wash.

9 Change your hours at work: new subway time, new gym time, new faces.

10 Volunteer for a good cause.

Does He Play the Odds Game? If you sense even for a second that he's trying to snare a woman, any woman, rather than trying to capture your heart specifically, run!

This is a guy who just wants a girlfriend. For him any woman will do. He's looking for a way to feel complete. Or worse, he's looking for a way to get laid! Some are easy to spot. We recognize their m.o. immediately or we've heard about them through the girls' club grapevine. They figure if they hit on enough women in the run of a day, they might get a date by Saturday night. No woman is immune to their well-worn pickup lines. From the bank teller to the meter maid, some men hit on 'em all. If they think they can score with one of every one hundred women they meet, then they are usually not fazed by a rejection from you. As soon as you say no, they move on to the other ninety-nine women they've targeted. We've all met these guys and there's a major downside to their game: High numbers mean faces become blurred.

There's a certain good-looking television reporter in Los Angeles who, over the years, has hit on me and one of my girlfriends on at least three separate occasions each! I swear this is true. Each time, he didn't recognize us. When I mentioned his antics to an older girlfriend who had gone to college with him, she said, "Oh, he hit on me at the beach twenty years ago." Yes, thankfully women remember and love to talk.

However, sometimes you don't have the benefit of guerrilla research. Sometimes you're approached by a guy you've never laid eyes on, or heard a bit of dirt on. For that you must depend on your highly evolved instincts.

Does He Work Too Fast?
After just a few minutes of conversation, before he knows much about you, this clueless Casanova will be begging for a date.

It's a known fact that most "odds players" work fast. If you're not going to fall for their lines, they want to know quickly so there's little time wasted and they can move on to the next target. If he asks you out before he knows what you do, what your interests are, and who you may know in common, be cautious. A serious boyfriend candidate will approach slowly and politely, looking for common ground. He wants to earn your trust and he's afraid of being rejected—after all, you are his Dream Girl and this first impression is very important to him.

This is called the pre-interview. In the first few minutes of small talk he should obtain enough information to know if asking for your phone number will get a positive result. There are basically three reasons why you shouldn't hand your phone number over to a strange man:

A. You're already in a relationship.

B. You don't trust him.

C. You're not attracted to him.

It amazes me that men forget to obtain this basic information before they give you their best shot. They blindly shoot the ball with no calculation. Before a good boyfriend candidate asks a woman for her number, he conducts a pre-interview designed to answer the ABCs of hooking up: (A) Is she available? (B) Does she feel safe with me? (C) Does she want to sleep with me?

Now, I'm not suggesting that your initial conversation should sound anything like this: "Hi. Do you have a boyfriend? 'Cause if you don't, I'm a really nice guy, and my mother will vouch for me. You know, I do a bit of modeling, and I have a big dick. Can I call you sometime?"

If I were the recipient of that sales pitch, I'd be running to my car faster than you can say Jeffrey Dahmer.

Instead, you should expect some small talk, smart small talk. Smart men don't ask you if you're in a relationship. Even if you're not, chances are you'll lie if he hasn't earned your trust (after all, down the road, you might need an out). Smart men chat for a while to gain your confidence, and watch your body language to see if you're physically attracted to them. Whether you're attached can be figured out through some intuitive detective work.

One guy friend of mine once saw a platonic female friend talking to a babe at the gym. He moved over to the two women on the pretense that he needed some real-estate advice from his friend, who was a realtor. At first he ignored the other woman, his potential Dream Girl, since he hadn't been formally introduced and he was playing it cool.

Instead he asked his friend how much she thought a renovation of his kitchen would increase the value of his house. Here he slyly added that that would be the only reason he'd do it since he rarely cooks or entertains. Bam! He had just sent three important messages to the babe: (1) He has a job, or at least a mortgage. Remember, the financial security gene is still alive in most of us. (2) He's available. Bachelors rarely entertain at home. (3) He's trustworthy. His friend, a girls' club member, is giving him the time of day.

Then it was his turn to get some information about her. He turned to her, said hello, and made a sweet, self-deprecating joke about how men are so dependent on women for guidance, and then asked her for her kitchen opinions. As she responded, he listened very closely to everything she said, and everything she didn't say, and most of all he listened to her body language. As she told him about her own kitchen renovation nightmares, she inadvertently slipped in a "we." Aha! A boyfriend or husband is—or was—on the scene.

But she also physically moved closer to him and unfolded her arms, letting him know she was attracted to him. A mixed message for sure. So he asked her what part of town she lived in. She named a suburb with predominantly single-family homes. He became suspicious. He's not dumb and stays away from other people's property. This could be a married woman looking for an affair. But then she added the most important piece of information so far: She mentioned that she was staying at her sister's house.

She didn't need to add that. It was a calculated move on her part. She was sending him the very important message that she was single. Now he had the answers to all three questions: (A) She's available. (B) She trusts him or she wouldn't be chatting in a such a friendly manner. And (C) she's physically attracted—the body language spoke enough.

Of course, my savvy guy friend knew that he'd be more attractive to her if he played hard to get. So even after a delightfully friendly conversation, he didn't ask for her phone number. He continued with his workout in another part of the gym, waiting to see if she chose to work out on machines in his vicinity and tried to catch his eye. She did. In the end he approached her and asked for her phone number in a very unobtrusive way.

On his way out he casually stopped to say good-bye. "I'm heading out now. Nice to have met you. Thanks for the advice on my kitchen. Hey, by the way, I'm leaving town for a couple weeks, but when I get back, would you like to have lunch?"

Read that subtext: "My workout's finished. I'm not hanging around the gym just to try to talk to you. I think you're smart and nice, and I'd like to have lunch (not dinner), but I'm in no urgent rush."

That's a smooth, disinterested game played by smart men, and it works every time if they've gotten the right answers in the pre-interview, and know their ABCs.

Does He Refuse to Take No for an Answer? Persistence is important in business. But there's a big difference between polite persistence and annoyance.

If he pressures you after you turn him down, watch out. This guy is very immature. A smart man will move off and try another tactic—say, a fix-up through a friend. But any guy who will try to wear you down isn't madly in love with you. Rather, he has a private battle to win.

One guy once sidled up beside me while I was manning a volunteer table at a charity event and very quickly asked me if I would have lunch with him. I politely told him that I was flattered but that I had a boyfriend. Later when I moved over to another task at the event, there he was again, asking me to reconsider. At this point he had exhibited three bad behaviors: He approached too fast, he didn't respect relationships, and he wouldn't take no for an answer. By the third time he asked me out, I had to be very clear and very firm. I simply asked, "If I was your girlfriend, would you want me to have lunch with another man?" I had to seriously spell it out for this guy. In the end he got it.

Is He Impaired When He Hits on You? Whether it's booze, drugs, or the endorphins from winning a marathon, if his judgment is impaired, don't give him your number.

The theory is this: After he comes down from his euphoria, he may find your phone number but have forgotten your face. Your number goes in the garbage and you sit by the phone. If he's a serious man and he finds your number, he'll probably be too embarrassed about his first impression and not call. Again you'll wonder why.

Case in point: A nice-looking professional athlete who played for the Lakers during their slump years once exchanged glances with me at a few games. One night during the season I visited a restaurant that a friend had purchased as an investment. Being near the University of Southern California at Los Angeles, the place attracted a rowdy college crowd, and it was there that I was surprised to spot my thirty-something athlete friend. He was obviously having a nostalgic moment partying with students from his old alma mater. Though surrounded by beer, boys, and breasts, he still made a beeline for me and eventually asked for my phone number. I stupidly gave it to him. Do you think he called? Not! To this day, I still wonder: Did he lose my number or did he throw it away out of embarrassment?

Does He Use a Stupid Pickup Line? If he resorts to bad attempts at humor, approaches you in a solemn manner that makes you feel uncomfortable, or uses any line that sounds rehearsed, eliminate him!

I've already said that the best pickup line is the word "Hi." Anything else is a big risk on his part. There is no such thing as a standard line that works on every woman. In fact, anything standard or rehearsed prompts us to ask ourselves, "Why isn't this guy being himself?"

During initial contact with a woman, a promising boyfriend candidate is basically trying to send the subliminal message that he respects and deserves the best. Also, that he sees women as more than sexual objects. With that in mind, there are certain ways a man can start a conversation that will score points on the Boyfriend Test

PICKUP LINES
That May Get a Good Grade

1 Hi. *(As long as he keeps moving as he utters this!)*

2 Excuse me. *(As he passes by.)*

3 You look like an attorney or doctor—what do you do?

4 I've been standing over there with my friends hearing too much guy talk. I need a fix of more stimulating conversation.

5 Did you see the news about [Mars landing, tobacco settlement, AIDS breakthrough, etc.]?

6 Any well-executed, good nonsexual joke that is guaranteed to get a laugh. *(Big risk here!)*

7 Do you want me to get rid of the jerk who's hounding you? *(After he does the chivalrous deed, he leaves!)*

(I should add that either I or my girlfriends have heard every one of these lines).

So that's the basics of meeting and greeting and disqualifying in the first heat. You are now ready for the Meet and Greet Report Card.

leet and Greet
Sheet Report Card

Note: This boyfriend candidate starts out with a rating of 50. From there his behavior either earns or loses him points.

1 Does he approach without an invitation?

___ Appears out of thin air (–10)
___ Answered your call of the wild (+10)

2 Does he refer to women as girls?

___ Yes (–10)
___ No (+10)
___ Not sure (0)

3 Is his focus your body over your brain?

___ Made no comment about your looks (+10)
___ Made one comment about your beauty in a polite, nonsexual manner (+5)
___ Made a comment about your looks using a veiled or overt sexual innuendo (-10)
___ Made more than one comment about your looks or body (–30)

4 Does he disrespect relationship boundaries?

___ Asked if you're seeing anyone else (+10)
___ You mentioned a boyfriend and he still proceeded with his come-on. (–15)
___ You mentioned a *husband* and he still continued his advances. (–50)
___ He didn't inquire about your status and you didn't give him any clues. (0)

5 Does he ignore workplace boundaries?

_____ This man is a colleague. (–5)

_____ This man is an underling. (–5)

_____ This man is in management at your company, though not your supervisor. (–25)

_____ This man is your boss. (–50)

6 Does he play the odds game?

This is impossible to test for unless you've heard or witnessed some past "numbers" game behavior.

_____ If so, give him –20.

_____ If you have no knowledge that he's an odds player and his behavior didn't give a hint of it, let him slide with five free points. (+5)

7 Does he work too fast?

_____ He seems in a hurry. (–10)

_____ He cuts to the chase with little small talk. (–5)

_____ He takes some time getting to know you before he asks you out. (+10)

8 Does he refuse to take no for an answer?

_____ He asks for a date a second time during the same conversation. (–10)

_____ He tried three times and it feels like pressure. (–25)

_____ You said "YES!" (0)

9 **Is he impaired when he hits on you?**

_____ He appears to have had a couple of drinks. (0)

_____ He seems kinda drunk. (–10)

_____ He's been ingesting more than alcohol. (–20)

_____ He's completely sober. (+5)

10 **Does he use a stupid pickup line?**

_____ He sounds rehearsed and insincere. (–10)

_____ He seems open and honest. (+5)

GRADING

Note: The candidate must score a minimum of a C+ for him to advance to the Telephone Test.

■ Exceptional (90–100) A+

So far this man looks like a possible roommate to your Barbie Dream house.

■ Excellent (80–89) A

This is a superb boyfriend candidate. Have a wonderful phone conversation.

■ Very Good (75–79) B+

This man makes very few mistakes. Watch on future parts of the test that his errors aren't crucial.

■ Good (70–74) B

Some men with this score on the Meet and Greet can pull their grades up on the Phone Test.

■ Satisfactory (65–69) C+

I do not recommend giving this guy a face-to-face chance. But if your beating heart can't stop you, be very cautious!

■ Minimum Pass (60–64) C

Barely post–Cro-Magnon. If you've given this man your number, you still don't have to go out with him. But if your smoldering loins can't stop you, be very, very cautious!

■ Failure (50–59) D

DO NOT ACCEPT THIS MAN'S PHONE CALL

■ Complete Failure (0–49) F

DO NOT GO OUT WITH THIS MAN UNDER ANY CIRCUMSTANCES!

the telephone test

> Good communication is stimulating as black coffee, and just as hard to sleep after.
> —Anne Morrow Lindbergh

At this point you have just met the man of your dreams. Or at least he's passed the first part of the Boyfriend Test: You've trusted him and like him enough to allow him to electronically converse with you.

And a quick word about your phone number. If you have even the slightest safety concern about handing your private home number to a stranger, *don't do it!* That's why God made pagers, cell phones, and office voice mail—to put you in control of who gets to you and when.

Also, I hope I don't have to remind you that the phone number should be passed from woman to man and not vice versa. It should be done upon his request only! Men are wired to chase women. In its most basic biological definition, sperm chase eggs in an effort to reproduce genes. It doesn't matter if intellectually most men cringe at the thought of fathering a screaming infant; biologically they can't help themselves.

And us girls' club members? Our eggs are sitting there waiting to take applications from racing sperm. In fact, anthropologists who study thousands of species sometimes have trouble telling the boys from the girls, and do so by examining the size of the sex cells. Their findings: Females have gigantic, almost stagnant eggs and males have a gazillion sprinting sperm. That's one of the reasons that men have big muscles, the better to chase women and fight off other male pursuers. In some other species, males even ejaculate a kind of combat sperm that kills off any rival sperm that may be lingering inside a female. And you thought all the wars were waged in the office!

In *Sex, Evolution, and Behavior*, evolutionary psychologists Martin Daly and Margo Wilson describe the genders' basic biology like this: "A sperm is an entity with a mission—search, find, fertilize. In intense competition with other sperms of similar ambitions, it has become stripped down and streamlined. As a participant in a race, it has jettisoned all nonessential baggage.... The prize for which the sperms compete is a relatively enormous gamete, the ovum, which does not move to welcome the victor but sluggishly awaits him."

So why do *you* move to welcome the victor? Stand your ground, girl. Let him ask for your phone number. While our evolution may have made us equally able to pick up the check, and survive on the planet, let me assure you, when it comes to reproduction, our sex cells haven't budged much. It is our job to coyly entice men, and their job to put in the miles. Need more proof? Check out a magazine rack. Women's magazines focus on adornment and nesting (*Glamour* and *Martha Stewart*), men's on sports and sex (*Sports Illustrated* and *Maxim*). Just ask any man, and he'll tell you he *loves* the chase, sometimes more than he loves the relationship, or even the sex. And he's a clueless idiot if he denies this.

I tested this rule only once in my life, and it was another humbling experience. After chatting on a couple of occasions with a fine-lookin' and smart-sounding boyfriend applicant at the gym, I defied my own rules and asked for his number. He gave it to me. When I called, I discovered that it was his cell phone number, not his home. This man didn't trust me! I found him in his car and we had yet another (or at least I thought) wonderfully stimulating conversation. In closing, we made plans to have dinner a few nights later. I then gave him my number and he told me he'd call me back to get my address. Do you think he called? *Not!* What's more, I have since run into him many times at the gym and he is still very sweet to me. I guess he likes the attention. But he has never suggested that we get together. Trust me and my girls' club members, no matter how liberated men are, if they think it's easy, they don't want it.

Now, down to the business of screening out the useless men on the telephone. Just because you've met a great boyfriend candidate and given him your phone number doesn't mean you have to go out with him. You're a busy Dream Girl. You don't need to waste your time. Begin the elimination process on the telephone.

QUESTION #1

Did He Take Too Long to Call? The industry standard is two to seven days. If he takes any longer, you should have forgotten his name.

I've been assured by all girls' club members that the most common time lapse between the number exchange and the number dialed is three days. Good boyfriends know that if they call any sooner, they could look a little too eager— remember, we like to do a bit of chasing, too, or at least we want to enjoy a small degree of anxiety about whether he's going to call. A Dream Man also knows that if he calls after a week, well, Dream Girl, you just may have been snapped up.

One friend of mine got a call from a guy who said he met her at my birthday party...eleven months before! He simply said he'd been thinking about her since then and wanted to get together. She called me to see if I could remember the dude. He must have been the guest of another friend, because I drew a complete blank. What was he thinking? Is she supposed to believe that she threw him into such a romantic tizzy that it took almost a year for him to get up the nerve to call? More likely he was in a relationship back then, and only now was free to call. But if that's true, why didn't he just say so? We're not stupid. We know there has to be a story there. This call made my friend suspicious. Perhaps he was an odds player who put her number in the pile and dug it up, along with some others, on a lonely, horny night. Yuck!

The bad boyfriends who are more difficult to spot with this telephone timing test are the ones who call just slightly over the limit. The seven-to-fourteen-day crowd are hard to screen out, especially if all you can recall about them is one set of dreamy brown eyes.

My advice: If he's someone who scored a big impression with you at your first meeting, cut him some slack here. But pay special attention to how he scores on the rest of the telephone test. Forgive him this one mistake, but *don't forget it*. The Boyfriend Test is designed to help you piece together a personality profile. And some guys are complicated jigsaw puzzles with dozens of tiny pieces.

QUESTION #2

Did He Call Too Soon? If this man can't even wait forty-eight

hours to hear your voice, he's not good at delaying gratification. Remember, someday this could be the man who has to wait months to have sex with you after you bear his child!

There's a great psychology best-seller called *Emotional Intelligence,* by Daniel Goleman, that illustrates how important the ability to delay gratification is. In this book, Goldman describes a very revealing "marshmallow" experiment, whereby four-year-old children were individually left alone in a room for five minutes with nothing to do but stare at a marshmallow sitting on a plate in front of them. The children were told that the adult would be back in five minutes, and if they didn't eat the marshmallow, they would be rewarded with two marshmallows, but if the marshmallow was gone, they would get nothing. When *60 Minutes* did this experiment using a cookie and hidden television cameras, the results were hilarious. In some cases, the door was barely closed behind the adult when the overzealous child would grab the cookie and stuff it in his mouth. In another case, the child carefully picked tiny crumbs off the cookie and put them in her mouth so her lack of self-control might go undetected. Still other children, deemed to be of high emotional intelligence, practiced techniques of distraction to wait out the five minutes. Some closed their eyes or drummed the table with their fingers, singing or dancing.

The theory proposed by psychologists is that those children

who passed the "marshmallow test" tended to grow up to be people who could put their nose to the grindstone, or the college books, and stick to something long enough to achieve it. They had great tenacity and were able to wait for life's rewards.

It's obvious how an ability to delay gratification can help one in business—taking time to do market research before pouring your life's savings into a new venture, for instance—as well as in other pursuits, like applying oneself to the years of schooling and training necessary in becoming a doctor.

But how about relationships? A good boyfriend needs this skill here, too. He'll have to delay gratification a few times to ride out all the bumps that come with a healthy, growing relationship. I mentioned the pregnancy issue. When I was in my first trimester of pregnancy, I was so nauseous that the thought of putting anything in my mouth made me gag. That included my man's body parts. For three months he stuck it out—or actually he didn't stick it out, he kept it in his pants. What a find!

Then he tested *my* ability to delay gratification. He asked me to wait until the birth of our child to find out the gender. Now, that was hard, especially because I had female decorating genes and nesting hormones and was dying to do the baby's room in the right colors. But I could wait because I'm a Dream Woman!

On the flip side, I once went out with a sexy, longhaired, TV star (who shall remain nameless) who couldn't get through three weeks on a film location without administering to his sexual urges. This was a problem since I was only able to visit the set every four weeks. The beneficiaries of my boyfriend's lack of ability to delay gratification included the makeup and wardrobe department. Yank their girls' club union cards, I say!

So if he calls you just minutes or hours after making your acquaintance, make a note of it. This could be one of the biggest indicators of his ability to have a healthy relationship.

Did He Call At an Inappropriate Hour? Appropriate hours for a first-time personal call are between nine A.M. and nine-thirty P.M. If he's not sensitive to your possible sleep needs, this man is not a keeper.

This guy is still a stranger and should show some degree of protocol in his early telephone manner. It doesn't matter if he's a sexy musician whose gig ends at two A.M. and you're the first thing he thinks about. Nor is it important if he's a free spirit who meditates at sunrise, a news anchor who goes into gear when the ten o'clock show wraps, or a traveling salesman in crazy time zones. The calling hours still apply if he's being considerate of you and your schedule. A Dream Man doesn't know what hours you keep, so he keeps it safe by following these guidelines.

Besides, with all the recent telephonic advances, a Dream Man doesn't know for sure what series of beeps, alarms, or rings his dialing those seven or ten digits creates. One friend of mine, a sales rep who's out of the office a lot, has her office voice mail ring her pager when a message arrives. And since she's usually in her car with Alanis Morrisette or Fiona Apple blaring at high decibels, her pager is set on loud, very loud, so pity the poor guy who thinks he's being cool by leaving a message at her office at five-thirty A.M. This, she tells me, happens from time to time, and when it does, don't put it past her to take the pager from her nightstand and throw it against the wall—and never return the phone call.

Or how about my friend whose mother is going through chemotherapy. Since she spends many nights at her sickbed, she forwards her home calls to Mom's line. Imagine the man who calls at eleven P.M., just minutes after the ailing woman has finally found relief in a REM zone. Dream Men are smart. They don't take risks like that.

Of course, polite calling hours don't have to be the rule for long. Once you and ole' Baritone Pipes have established a certain telephone rapport, tell him what times you'd prefer to receive calls. Perhaps the two of you are insomniac soul mates and love to chat at three A.M. If so, go for it!

Okay, so assuming the game of telephone tag has been relatively brief (long games of telephone tag often mean the man would rather *not* connect with you), now is your chance to peel some layers to reveal his personality.

Does He Give Good Phone?

Conversation is the way to a woman's heart. Bad boyfriends want to cut to the chase and set up a date, with little verbal enticement.

Every woman knows a man who stole her heart on the telephone. He was thoughtful. He was funny. He was stimulating. You couldn't wait to spend time with him in person. We all know the route to our vaginas is through our head, and the phone can be one giant vibrator. I don't mean to imply that phone sex is cool early on. I mean that smart, humorous men are very sexy. When you finally do sit across from him in a restaurant, after a high-energy intelligent phone conversation, he'll look to you like Brad Pitt, no matter who he is.

In *Soul Mates,* writer and philosopher Thomas Moore writes, "True conversation is an interpenetration of worlds, a genuine intercourse of souls, which doesn't have to be self-consciously profound but does have to touch matters of concern to the soul."

Good men know that you may not trust them after only a quick meeting. But they should *try* to earn your trust on the phone. This is a sales pitch, so let him interview you or just charm you with delightful small talk. However, when he speaks, listen not just to what he says, but to what he omits.

Did He Seem Vague? He gives only fillers, no facts. He dances around some of your personal questions. This guy is hiding something!

Hiding a wife, perhaps? Or a prison record? Go ahead and laugh, my savvy women of the millennium, but listen to this one: At a recent charity dinner, a charming man from San Francisco was seated between two girlfriends of mine. One, he openly flirted with. The other he talked business to all night, after she told him she was looking to make a career move. The evening ended with him giving some kissy-face in an elevator to the girlfriend he had flirted with. (Shame on her!) He had also exchanged phone numbers with the other girlfriend on a business pretense—and I stress the word *pretense!*

The next week he phoned the kissing girlfriend and said he was coming into town for one night only and would love to take her to dinner. She accepted. The day of the dinner, she happened to be speaking with my other friend and mentioned that the Bay Area babe was coming to town. Imagine her surprise when the other woman told her she was aware of that fact because he had invited *her* to dinner for the following night. (You have to question her girls' club ethics. She knew the kissing girlfriend had a crush, and she still made a dinner date with him. However, according to club rules, she assured her pal that *her* dinner was to be all business.)

Enter Mr. San Francisco. Of course, he swept ole kissy-face off her feet and by dessert was suggesting they head to his hotel room. That was when my Dream Girl found her head and dropped a sly bombshell. She told him she had to make it an early night, but if he was going to be in town for one more night, perhaps they could meet then. Can you believe he stuck to his lie that he had to catch an early plane out!

Cut to the next evening. Dinner number two. Woman number two. Surprise, surprise. He seemed to have forgotten his corporate agenda and spent more time talking about her legs than her résumé.

Obviously neither girlfriend took his phone calls after that—that is, after they placed a conference call and busted him! But there's even more to this story. A third Bay Area girlfriend called with the results of some guerrilla research: The guy was married with children. Creep!

Not to single out my girlfriends. I've fallen for some doozies, too. Upon interviewing one potential boyfriend, I noticed a conspicuous hole in his résumé. There was a one-year gap where he mentioned nothing about business or girlfriends. In response to my questions about it, he said he had taken some time off to travel but didn't elaborate on where. When pushed for it, he just replied, "Europe," and then changed the subject. This big omission kind of nagged at me for a while. Who doesn't gush with details after spending a year in Europe? It prompted me to do some serious asking around, specifically about his whereabouts during that time period.

And I found the answers. Are you ready? Prison. Drug

charge. Yep. I met him just weeks after his release. Okay, I admit it, after a year in jail, the sex was great! But his potential to be a responsible boyfriend was seriously lacking.

So while it's important to listen to what men say, it's far more important to hear what they don't say. And some losers can be very sneaky when it comes to hiding their weaknesses. A smart Dream Girl should eventually take control of the phone interview.

I usually let him begin the conversation. Even great boyfriend candidates rehearse a couple of thoughts they can use to start off the gabbing. Let him work his material a bit first.

Jokes are always good, but listen to what's underneath too much self-deprecating humor. One joke about his shiny bald spot is cute. It makes him look humble. Three jokes about it, and you know he's got a complex. Remember, all comedy is simply tragedy viewed from across the street, and a big truth lies behind every small joke.

One successful L.A. lawyer I know likes to joke about being a poor Jewish boy from Brooklyn. At first it really is quite humorous. Who could imagine this well-dressed, educated, world-savvy veteran as an impoverished son of immigrants? But a woman doesn't need to spend much time with him to see that he really does feel inadequate about his roots, and the "poor Jewish boy" shtick becomes an excuse for his perceived failings.

This is not to say that you should hang up on every guy who has issues. We *all* have issues. Yes, Dream Girl, even you. The test is to find out how conscious he is of his issues or how comfortable he is discussing them. This is not to suggest that a first phone call should transcend into a psychotherapy session, but you shouldn't be afraid to gingerly probe this guy's life motivations. (You knew that Psych 101 course would come in handy someday!)

One question I have learned to ask early on is simple yet revealing: "Do you have a girlfriend?"

I know you're assuming he's single if he's asked for your number, but you're underestimating the snakes out there. Of course, bad boyfriend candidates will lie to you and claim they don't have a girlfriend, so it's imperative that you follow up with, "Let me rephrase my question. Is there any person out there who *thinks* she's your girlfriend?"

Good guys always find that a clever question. Bad ones get defensive. Either they're angry that you're accusing them of lying or they're angry because they're busted. In any case, this question often prompts some interesting replies.

Next phone topic: news and current events. No, not the weather! You're trying to find out if this guy reads anything outside of *Sports Illustrated,* not if he can look out a window. Dream Men read. Some have even read some of your favorite books, too.

You don't have to be searching for Einstein, just a man who's aware. A guy who's not trapped in Shaq worship, going on religious retreats to Hooters to watch reruns of *Baywatch.* While I've said that men are visually attuned, and being a sports fan isn't a bad thing, we also hope that's not *all* they are. Talking about current events will help you determine this.

And a red light should go off if your guy isn't interested in lengthy conversation but just wants to set up a time to see you. This could be another odds player. It's true, men are visually attuned and should want to see you again ASAP; Dream Men will do what it takes to earn your confidence.

QUESTION #6

Does He Want to See You That Night? If he catches you during the day and asks you out for that same evening, any women worth her self-esteem will not accept the date.

Back to that ability to delay gratification. Why would a guy ever call a woman up and ask to see her just hours later? No discipline. Besides, men don't really want a woman who's completely available (read: not worth it).

One friend of mine, a bright young accountant, once got a phone call at 8:45 on a Friday night from a man she'd recently met, a business manager who specializes in athletes and actors. He wondered if she was available for a late dinner. She paused, took a deep breath, and glanced at her television screen. She had muted the sound when she took the phone call, but now my friend quickly surfed the local stations with her remote control. When she found what she had suspected, she quietly said, "Are you watching the Celtics game?"

Taken off guard and impressed that she might be a sports fan, he quickly answered, "Yes."

Then the witty and wise young woman, who had done her guerrilla research and discovered the man was a bit of an odds player, said, "I get the picture here. You're at home on your couch. It's Friday night. It's halftime. You're getting a little hungry, so you pull out your Palm Pilot phone book, and amazingly halftime isn't even over yet and you got to the K's. I feel so special."

The guy was so taken aback that his game strategy had been revealed that he freaked out and hung up the phone. Of course, not all men are so crafty....

By the way, men also don't necessarily want you to cancel any plan at the drop of the hat to make one with them. At least normal, self-confident men don't.

But beware the high-pressure man who really tries to convince you to change your prior obligations for him. He could be dangerous. One guy who seemed obsessed with getting me to cancel my plans for him said things like "C'mon, the guy's probably a jerk. Go out with me. I'll show you a better time."

The psychological subtext of this kind of talk is "I'm aroused by the idea of competing with another guy because I have something to prove. I want to like myself better." I wouldn't go out with the guy who tried this tactic on me. And I didn't tell him that my "plans" were to soak in a tub and read a book.

Unfortunately, I also didn't take my own advice and reject this particular guy early on. Weeks later, after some inconsistent dating behavior that would have failed the Boyfriend Test, he turned up at my door late one night. I let him in and was met with some unwanted hard-core sexual advances. He even said, "I have to have you tonight, after I saw you on TV this evening interviewing Eddie Murphy. Tell me the truth. Did you put out for Eddie?"

I was shocked! In one moment I had become someone's conquest. What's more, my value as a sexual target had gone up when he thought I had been carousing with a celebrity. His own insecurities about other men to whom he felt "less than" ruled his behavior.

The guy was six foot five, 230 pounds, and not happy to hear the word *no.* I think I was lucky to have gotten out of the situation safely that night. But enough about that. (And by the way, Mr. Murphy had been nothing but professional in his conduct.)

QUESTION #7

Does He Have a Plan? If he calls for a date and has no idea what he's inviting you to, he's a bad boyfriend bet.

Whether it's dinner, a game, a museum, or whatever, great boyfriend candidates have ideas. Nothing makes a woman crazier than a man without a plan. Dream Men send us the message that they've got a full life and would like to include us in it one night. His inquiry should sound something like "I have tickets next Tuesday to the Red Sox game. Would you like to go?" Or "I just read a review of this new Italian restaurant. I'm going to try it on Saturday night. Would you like to go?"

The implication in both cases is that he'll be going anyway, whether you're available or not. While he'd like your company, it's not imperative.

It's okay if he says, "Do you like sushi?" But if he follows up with, "Do you know of any good sushi restaurants?" he's losing points fast. I mean, who's chasing whom here? I usually respond to those questions with, "I dunno. You call the shots. Figure something out."

Dream Men have a mission. They take a direction. They are fast-swimming sperm in courting rituals. If a man makes you social director on the first date, you can be sure that you will be saddled with the responsibility forever if he goes on to become your boyfriend.

Does He Call More Than Once Before a First Date?

Dream Men call once, have a plan in mind, set the time, and get directions to your house. The next ring you hear should be your doorbell.

Idiots forget to get important information. Losers lose your information. Dorks look for excuses to call you again before the date. They can't wait to see you. Here we are again with that delayed gratification issue. I know I'm harping on it, but it's vital to an evolved relationship.

Smart men exchange all the information they need during that initial phone call. They know it's risky to call you again. They might look too eager or it may give you an opportunity to cancel. One guy friend of mine even went so far as to turn off his answering machine for an entire week so his date couldn't call back and cancel. Now, that idea is a bit extreme, but it worked. When he picked her up, she said she had been trying to get in touch with him about "rescheduling."

On that first and only phone call, Dream Men get your exact address and write it down correctly. One girlfriend told me that she loves it when men simply take down the address and decline street directions, saying, "Don't worry, I'll find it." This sends a message to a woman that he's a smart man, can read maps, and is not afraid of a little detective work, especially if you're the prize.

QUESTION #9

Does He Try to Give You Fashion Tips? Short of informing you of any dress codes, men shouldn't try to give women fashion advice.

On that initial phone call, after you have accepted his invitation, a Dream Man will tell you what time he'll be picking you up and then quickly mention any dress requirements. He won't make a big deal about this. You know he's considerate if he politely adds, "Bring a coat. Hockey arenas can get cold." Or "This charity event is blacktie optional. I'll be wearing a suit rather than a tux." This will keep you from wearing a floor-length dress and feeling awkwardly overdressed beside him.

Simple wardrobe advice, when it's not "Please wear something short and tight," we can handle. On the other hand, be wary of the man who speaks as if he's trying to control and change you before you've even had a chance to get to know him. So unless he works in the fashion industry—in women's apparel!—wardrobe suggestions should be a major "heads-up" that this guy could be controlling, or he treats women like objects, or has a whore/madonna complex and is trying to make you one or the other.

I mentioned a strappy shoe lover before. He saved me from another. At the close of one delightfully entertaining first conversation I had a couple years ago, a perspective date fouled himself by asking if I owned any strappy high-heeled pumps, and would I wear them on the date? Busted! I knew what this meant this time. He had just revealed a foot fetish way too early in the relationship and made me feel like my toes were more important to him than my soul. Of course, I gave him a verbal cold shower by exclaiming that I suffered from ugly bunions and corns and wouldn't be caught dead in strappy shoes.

Does He Try More Than Twice? This isn't a baseball game. If a Dream Man gets turned down twice, he proudly saunters back to the dugout. Your team is now up at bat.

If you decide to decline his invitation, be nice about it. Great guys believe it when you say you have other plans. Great women who have a direction in life don't spend a lot of time sitting at home washing their hair.

However, don't fault him if he tries just one more time. Dream Men aren't afraid to be a little persistent. But beware the phone man who calls every week for six weeks. Yes, it's flattering, but it's also kind of creepy. You should ask yourself, Why isn't this guy smart enough to get the message?

On the second pitch, Dream Men follow the same rules as the first call, except they might try to stay on the phone a little longer to gain your trust. If you're unavailable the second time because of conflicting schedules, a good boyfriend candidate will be nice about it and may simply leave you his number. No man should have to strike out three times, so the ball is probably in your court at this point.

Grading the Test Taker

On page 155 you'll find a report card for the Telephone Test. I encourage you to fill it out in detail and rely on your gut, especially in regard to those questions about vagueness.

Your challenge is to decide when an honest, clueless mistake is really the mark of a self-loathing, not-ready-for-a-relationship hunk, and for that you have to rely on your God-given intuition.

Luckily you are a woman. You have inherited insight and gut instincts that most men would covet. It makes sense that it is the female gender who evolved with a heightened intuitive ability. Men's ancestral role was to hunt and patrol the perimeter of the encampment, clobbering any menacing enemy or animal who might threaten to kill his offspring. For that he needed a poker face, some adrenaline, and the ability to get really mad without warning. Sound like any man you know?

For our genes to survive, our ancestral mothers needed to decipher the needs of a crying or listless infant who couldn't utter a word of useful language. We were forced to pay attention to facial expressions, body language, smells, temperature, vocal tones—anything that might give us a clue as to what that tiny human being required to survive.

Lately, as we've come to depend on science so much, we've grown to distrust anything intangible or immeasurable like a "gut feeling." But I assure you, you have a secret power! Call it empathy, intuition, insight, psychic ability, instinct, whatever. It's your ability to really know what's in the mind of a man. I encourage you to tap into your ancestral wisdom. It is your most prized asset.

Of course, it's hard to hear the truthful messages over the din of denials in your head, denials that sound like this: "He made one wrong move, so he's out!" or "He made nine bad moves, but I'm sure he's a really nice guy underneath." Both notions are irrational. Those denials are created by insecurity or desperation, and boil down to a kind of fear...fear of treading into the uncharted waters of an evolved relationship.

Happiness Can Be Frightening

Let me break it down for you. Things that are unfamiliar to us are frightening, even if they have the potential to improve our lives. This includes healthy relationships. Happiness can be a scary thing, especially if we've never experienced it. And a happy relationship may be the most foreign thing we've ever seen.

Top that off with the fact that early in life we were programmed to pattern most of our opposite-gender relationships on the one we had with our fathers (or even mothers), who may not have been the perfect role models or ideal. That leaves us to scramble around focusing on our careers, ignoring biological destiny, and dating many hurtful men!

The guidelines of the Boyfriend Test can help jump-start your powers of intuition and help you create healthy boundaries. There are times for many of us when we should *not* trust our own feelings. Our own feelings may tell us to run from a man who may bring us love, or tolerate a man who brings us a familiar unhappiness. While some women (the few who had great parents who had evolved marriages) might read this book and say, "Duh!," most of us will say, "Hmmm. I knew that, I just never thought about it before."

Well, think about it. You're about to go out on a first date with the new you. Be sure of how you like to be treated. Set clear boundaries in your head, and yes, stick to the Boyfriend Test as your guideline.

Don't Defend Bad Behavior!

If you have given a man your phone number, it's because he fulfills the majority of your desires at the time. When you evaluate him on the Meet and Greet and the Telephone Tests, you must not cloud your grading with superficial rationalizations of his bad behavior.

That means you can't say, "Well, he wasn't very verbal on the phone, and he did make a joke about my love of opera, and oh yes, he did refer to his most recent ex as the girlfriend from Hell, but he was sooo gorgeous and he was suffering from jet lag since he just flew in from Europe." Girlfriend, don't make excuses for him, and don't go out with him.

It's true that men may lie when trying to conquer a female. They say they'll call when they don't. They say we're the only one they're seeing. They even say they love us when their behavior demonstrates anything but. But why do we waste energy trying to understand them, when we could just be moving on?

Research on dishonesty, done by Dr. Dory Hollander, found women and men differ in their reactions to being lied to. In her book *101 Lies Men Tell Women and Why Women Believe Them,* Dr. Hollander says that when a woman is lied to, she most likely will "deny the lie, blame herself (not the liar), endlessly replay the circumstances of the lie, or want to discuss what happened. A man lied to is more likely to confront the liar, find the lie amusing, and/or terminate the relationship."

So my advice is: Give them a taste of their own medicine— confront, laugh, and terminate.

I used to be very good at making excuses for bad behavior. Case in point: Back in my twenties, when I was young and naive (I'm prefacing this story with a disclaimer because you're about to hear about a huge mistake), I had a promising Meet and Greet with a man who proceeded to fail the Telephone Test miserably.

This man was so tall and sexually attractive that I could barely stand next to him without feeling faint. In addition he was a self-made success. He owned a real-estate development company and drove a brand-new Mercedes convertible. Top it off with the fact that he had this bad-boy edge (read: irresponsible behavior bent), and I was lusting after him like a fish to bait.

His first phone call to me came at two A.M.! I'm not kidding. I was in a dead sleep on a Saturday night and the ringing of the damn phone interrupted my sweet dreams. My first mistake was to pick it up at all. That's what GTE voice mail is made for. But I did.

Still, because he had so many winning, though superficial,

attributes, I rationalized his bad behavior. I told myself that since I usually left the newsroom around eleven-thirty P.M., he would have known that I would still be awake at two o'clock, which, of course, I wasn't. But wait. It gets worse. He was calling from his car on the way home from a nightclub and asked if I would join him for a nightcap.

And I consented, telling myself that sometimes the most creative and intelligent people are night owls! Was there a chance in hell that this date could amount to anything more than a booty call? Of course not.

I was ignoring all the red lights while focusing on his body. His car. His job. His deep voice. His hearty, confident laugh. Hell, in my fantasies, I was already decorating model homes for his company! In short, I was focusing on all the wrong aspects of this man, on the potential of the relationship rather than the obvious facts.

The end of the story is predictable. Yes, he was slightly impaired that night. Yes, he was looking for sex. No, he never became a boyfriend to me or, as the grapevine tells me, to anyone else. And I definitely never got to choose so much as a couch for our model home.

One other note: Your highly evolved female psyche is clever. Very clever. When you grade your man, you may unconsciously be practicing "selective hearing." When you *want* a man to pass the test, your very smart brain may fool you into believing that he truly *is* passing the test. That's why you have to remain clear, conscious, and unforgiving.

The Boyfriend Test highlights specific behaviors that indicate whether a man is kind, compassionate, intelligent, and has the ability to love. You have to trust it. You have to use it honestly, and you must be strong enough to eliminate those who fail along the way.

Getting Rid of Him

A note about the turndown. I have learned that many women do not know how to kindly reject a man, so they play the deflection game by always saying they are "busy." This can send a mixed signal to men. They know they're being turned down, but they are also unconsciously being told it's okay to try again. This can create that crazy anxiety induced by those manipulative "Rules" girls.

If you're looking for a man who is honest and respectful of your feelings, you must treat every man the same way. No matter how much ego-boosting you get out of a bunch of answering machine messages from men you don't really want to go out with, you must be kind and cut them loose.

In surveying my boys' club friends, I have been told that the way most men prefer to be turned down is with the "Sorry, I have a boyfriend" line. One friend told me that his favorite rejector also added, "I *wish* I could go out with you, but I hope you'll respect that I can't." He walked away with his ego barely bruised on that one. By the way, he *swears* she meant it.

This line also comes in handy because it reveals those guys who don't respect relationships and continue to persist even after you've mentioned a boyfriend. However, it's a line that loses power if you have chatted for thirty minutes, given a guy your number, and then suddenly "remembered" you have a boyfriend.

The true genius of communication is in being completely kind and at the same time completely honest. This takes self-confidence and compassion. So suck it up, my dear, and tell him the truth. Here are some samples of rejections that have worked for me when a guy's asked me out after a failure of the Telephone Test:

✔ You seem like a really nice person, and you're certainly cute, but somehow I don't think romance is in the cards for us.

✔ To tell you the truth, I've enjoyed talking to you, but in all fairness, my work life is so hectic right now that I don't feel that I can apply the needed energy to even a dating relationship.

✔ You know, I really don't want to waste your time or your money, so I think it's best that we don't go out.

✔ We definitely have some synergy, but I'd prefer we keep it more professional than personal.

> ✔ You are such an interesting guy, I hope that you will only take this as a compliment, but I'd like to introduce you to a girlfriend who I think might be a better match.

> ✔ I'm obviously physically attracted to you or I wouldn't have given you my number, but I think our lifestyles are so very different that it would be really frustrating for us to attempt a romance.

By the way, I used that last one with a guy I had two conversations with. During each I inquired about the baby I heard crying in the background. He informed me that they were two different babies I had heard, both his children from different girlfriends. Yep, that's a lifestyle clash for me.

I realize there's a little "ouch!" in all of those speeches, but if spoken kindly with a soft voice, directly from the heart, a confident man will understand. A final reminder: The world's most powerful aphrodisiac is the word *no,* so be prepared to repeat your turndown line on subsequent phone calls. This kind of sweet rejection sometimes makes men try harder. Hold your ground, girl. Stay strong. And don't be afraid to become very firm and brutally honest if you have to.

The Telephone Test
Report Card

Note: Each boyfriend candidate starts with a new rating of 50. From there his behavior either earns or loses him points.

1 Did he take too long to call?

___ 1–2 days (see Question #2) (0)
___ 2–7 days (+10)
___ 8–14 days (+5)
___ More than two weeks! (–10)

2 Did he call too soon?

___ One hour or less after obtaining your number (–10)
___ Within six hours (–8)
___ Six to twelve hours (–6)
___ Twelve to twenty-four hours (–4)
___ Twenty-four to forty-eight hours (0)
___ He didn't call too soon. (+5)

(2a) Telephone Test Bonus Points

___ He called when he *said* he was going to call. (+5)
___ He promised to call on a certain date and called on a later date. (–25)

3 Did he call at an inappropriate hour?

___ 9:00 A.M. to 9:30 P.M. (+10)
___ 7:00 A.M. to 9:00 A.M. (–6)
___ 9:30 P.M. to 10:30 P.M. (–4)
___ 10:30 P.M. to 12:00 midnight on a Friday or Saturday. (–8)

_____ 10:30 P.M. to 12:00 midnight on a weeknight (–10)

_____ Midnight to 7 A.M. (–30)

4 Does he give good phone?

_____ Asked more than two questions about you (+2)

_____ Seemed thoughtful (+2)

_____ Seemed funny (+2)

_____ Appeared to listen well (you didn't have to repeat anything you already told him at the first meeting) (+2)

_____ Had good phone manners regarding call waiting or work interrruptions (i.e., didn't scream at coworkers in the background, "Shut up, I'm tryin to talk!") (+2)

_____ Made at least one derogatory comment (even as a joke) about you, your hometown, your job, your hobbies, etc. (–15)

_____ Made at least one derogatory comment about any of his ex-girlfriends (–20)

5 Did he seem vague?

Subtract points if he seemed skittish or insincere about:

_____ His job (–5)

_____ His leisure time (–5)

_____ His family of origin (–5)

_____ His relationship history (–5)

_____ His current relationship status (–25)

6 Does he want to see you that night?

____ Asks about your availability for that very evening (–15)

____ Wants to go out tomorrow night (–10)

____ Books a date for three to seven days in advance (+10)

____ Is unable to see you for more than a week (–4)

____ Is unable to see you for more than two weeks (–7)

____ Can't see you for one to two weeks because of a previously arranged trip, but makes up for it by calling or e-mailing at least once from his hotel (+5)

7 Does he have a plan?

____ Created a detailed plan but with no flexibility (+8)

____ Provided two good choices, both of which had been researched and/or reserved (+10)

____ Had a good idea but hadn't researched it (+5)

____ Asked you to join a group of his friends (–3)

____ Asked pertinent questions about you in order to make an informed decision (e.g., What part of town do you live in? Do you like sushi? Are you a sports fan, vegetarian, or theater lover?) (+5)

____ Suggested a sporting event, action flick, or other "guy"-oriented activity (–6)

____ Clearly had no idea what to do or where to go and was looking for you to fill in the blanks (–15)

8 Does he call more than once before a first date?

_____ Did not call again before the date (+10)

_____ Called only because important information had changed about the date (e.g., new meeting location, unable to get promised reservation, weather watch, etc.) (–5)

_____ Called to change the time or date because of a conflict he had (loses points even if he says it's business) (–8)

_____ Called to confirm information you had already given him (–15)

9 Does he try to give you fashion tips?

_____ He made no comment about attire, unless you asked. (+10)

_____ Without your inquiry, he mentioned a dress code or weather issue. (+5)

_____ He didn't _tell_ you what to wear, but he mentioned his favorite "style" for women. (–10)

_____ He asked you to wear something specific. (–20)

10 Does he try more than twice?

_____ When you weren't available, he tried one more time, at least a week later. (+10)

_____ When you weren't available, he didn't call back and it's been fourteen days. (–25)

_____ When you turned him down, he was polite about it. (+5)

_____ When you turned him down, he made a negative remark. (–15)

_____ When you still weren't available, he tried a third time! (–20)

_____ If you were available first time around, let him slide with ten free points. (+10)

GRADING

Note: This grade is calculated by adding the scores from the Meet and Greet and the Telephone Test and then dividing by two.

The candidate must have an average of B to advance to the First Date Test.

■ Exceptional (90–100) A+

Prince Charming he may very well be.

■ Excellent (80–89) A

This is a superb boyfriend candidate. Have a wonderful first date.

■ Very Good (75–79) B+

This man makes very few mistakes. Watch on future parts of the test that his errors aren't crucial.

■ Good (70–74) B

Plenty of men with this score on the Telephone Test pull their grades up on a face-to-face oral exam.

■ Satisfactory (65–69) C+

Do not give this guy a face-to-face chance.

■ Minimum Pass (60–64) C

Barely post–Cro-Magnon. If you've set up a date with this man, cancel it and go have a massage.

■ Failure (50–59) D

You might want to consider changing your phone number.

■ Complete Failure (0–49) F

DO NOT GO OUT WITH THIS MAN UNDER ANY CIRCUMSTANCES! Change your phone number if you have to.

the first-date test

> I shall be poised and cool and remember that I am a woman of substance and do not need men in order to be complete, especially not him.
>
> —Helen Fielding, *Bridget Jones's Diary*

A hh, the first date. What a make-or-break occasion. If he's passed the first two phases of the Boyfriend Test, your anticipation should now be peaking. The big night is finally here, a first date with your potential Man—with a capital *M*. How exciting!

As you paint your face and choose your clothes, you should have endorphins running through your veins like you would if you'd just completed the Eco-Challenge. If you don't, I ask you, should you be going out with this man? Maybe you're just filling time. Trust me, if this guy's not ringing your dinner bell, your time would be better spent reading a book, doing volunteer work, or sweating in a kick-boxing class.

On the other hand, if he *is* a potential Dream Man, it's okay to be a bit nervous. Physiological symptoms like an increased heart rate, sweaty palms, and shortness of breath mean you're being stimulated by him. That's good. Once I was on the phone with the actor James Woods and was busted when he asked if I was smoking! I guess I'd gotten so out of breath that a Hollywood leading man had called, that my attempt to obtain more oxygen made it sound as if I was sucking on a cigarette.

Whether you're eighteen or eighty, preparing for first dates is a fun challenge. They evoke feelings similar to those we had before our first school recital or our high-school prom. It can be a great high. And here comes another word of caution: Is this your drug? Are you a serial dater who, like many men, gets high off the chase but shrinks away from true emotional intimacy? If so, this might be a good time to analyze your motives and reflect on past behavior patterns. Think about the last time you felt this way. How did it eventually turn out? How long did it take you to realize that he wasn't the great guy you thought he was?

Such thoughts can put a damper on your current infatuation with his potential, but remember, potential can't love you back! Enjoy the high of a first date, but rein it in just enough to see truth and reality and not just your romantic expectations.

With first dates, even the most liberated of us still fall prey to our culture's pressure to look like a sex goddess. Here's a little advice: It's more important to *feel* like a sex goddess than look like one. I promise you he'll get your vibe. Also, keep a level head, girlfriend. Your sexual power is not something to be denied, but your emotional and intellectual power will be far more valuable to you if this date is going to evolve into a relationship. Remember, kindness and intelligence are first on the list of men's desires.

This is also the time to be extra cautious. You may be about to add the physical element. Sometimes it's hard to hear anything when your thoughts are transfixed on a future earth-shattering orgasm.

Don't Forget That You're the One Doing the Interviewing

We all like to be liked. It's nice to win over people and feel accepted—and maybe even loved—by them. But don't put aside the fact that you are the one doing the choosing. You are the interviewer. You are the gatekeeper to your heart. And you are deciding whether you like *him.*

Of course, a date is a distinct kind of interview. Unlike a job interview, an examination at the INS, or an interrogation by a police officer, "dates" have to be polite. If you show up primed with a mental list of questions and execute them in the prescribed order, you will be about as welcome as a *60 Minutes* camera crew.

Dates are about two people making "nice-nice" to disguise

their frailties. An unwritten rule about all first dates is that they be cordial, rosy, and filled with laughter. They are us living out our best fantasy of how we want to be perceived. It is a fleeting moment in our lives. Not surprisingly, many people are addicted to the first few dates and despair when, not so many dates down the road, humanity rears its imperfect head.

But if all this "nice-nice" is the tone of the evening, how do you discover anything of substance? Well, it happens in small ways. Tiny observances and sly inquiries are your heart's insurance policy.

QUESTION #1

Is He a Stickler About Transportation? Be cautious about the man who doesn't allow you your own getaway vehicle or, on the other hand, expects you to get there yourself.

While a man should always offer to provide transportation, he should also respect your desire to arrive solo. If he insists on doing the driving, sharing the cab, or taking the train together, even though you've expressed a desire to have some independent mode of transportation, you must wonder if a reflex to control is part of his psyche.

I do recommend that you meet at a public place on any first date, no matter who introduced you. It makes sense in this day of high crime and disillusioned humans. I have a friend whose *mother* set her up with a "nice young man" who turned out to be a drug addict who became impaired during dinner! She certainly wasn't thrilled about the idea of a ride home with him at the wheel.

Of course, there may be some practical reasons why he won't want you to drive—he has only one parking pass at the stadium, for example, or his out-of-the-way restaurant has tedious directions—so this is your first opportunity to be assertive and state your needs, by suggesting an alternate venue. While I mentioned before that this man should have a plan, he should also be flexible and considerate of your needs. A rigid man is not what we need.

So as to not compromise the "nice-nice" required of first dates, rather than saying, "I don't trust you enough to be in a car alone with you," choose a more diplomatic approach. Steer him to a restaurant that you are familiar with by simply asking, "May I suggest a place?" This is sweet. It will be perceived as demure. What guy is going to say, "No, I need to be in charge, here"? Only the one you shouldn't go out with.

Besides events where you are a hostage of his car, I also believe that you should avoid dark movie theaters or loud concerts on a first date. Remember, you're trying to get to know him. How can that be done without the magic of language?

On the other hand, this candidate may not even offer to drive and assumes you will meet him somewhere. Please respect yourself and call him on this one. I live in sprawling Los Angeles, where people can be G.U. (geographically undesirable) within the same city. But great men still *offer* to pick women up even if it means a forty-five- or sixty-minute journey across town (whether you accept the offer is your business).

One girlfriend of mine lives in the northeast part of the city, Pasadena, and a man she met at a party lives in the southwest corner of the city, Long Beach. When he called to ask her out, she said she preferred to meet at a restaurant near her house. He drove almost an hour, met her for a forty-five-minute date (she declined dessert), and then drove back home. She learned at dinner that the chemistry wasn't there for her. He took a big gamble and lost. But those are the breaks of being a man. After all, it is *his* job to pursue. It was her job not to mislead. She didn't want to waste more of his time and money once she'd decided that they were incompatible.

QUESTION #2

Does He Veer from His ETA?
Whether too early or too late, this man's arrival time says something about him.

There are many excuses for being late on a first date. His boss could have delayed him. The dry cleaners might not have had his shirt ready. The traffic could have been bad. His dog could have eaten the directions. But that's all they are—excuses.

A prepared person, one who is anticipating a big event, is never late. Years ago I remember seeing an episode of the now-defunct Phil Donahue talk show, where he was illustrating how anticipation can motivate by using an example from his own childhood. He said that when he was sick as a child he loved to stay home from school, but there were certain days, like a field trip day, when no matter how sick he was, he had a miraculous recovery, and even showed up early.

A date with you is a field trip day. You should expect him to treat it that way. Bosses can be manipulated, traffic can be anticipated, canines can eat Alpo, and this man can be on time for you.

Now, let's talk about the fine art of clock watching. What if this man is a few minutes early? Is he just being prepared or is he overzealous? I'd veer toward the trying-too-hard side. Even if a man arrived early because he couldn't predict the traffic, a smart man will kill time on the street, in his car, or at a coffee shop, before barging in on a woman in full makeover mode.

So what about those guys who are exactly on time—to the minute? The word *fastidious* comes to mind, as does the more common colloquial term anal-retentive. A guy like that is one step up from the early birds, but you've still got to question his coolness or wonder about his ability to be flexible with your schedule once you're his girlfriend.

A cool guy shows up five minutes late. It's not tardy enough for you to get angry, but it is just late enough for you to wonder for a few seconds if he's going to show. Even this tiny piece of anxiety will work in his favor. He's the chaser hoping you'll forget that fact and turn to pursue him.

Any more than five or six minutes late and this guy loses

points. Whether he's disorganized, not respectful of your schedule, or hoping to fail, this man is setting a very bad first impression. And if you let it slide, you'll be sending him the message that it's okay to be treated that way.

Some chronically late men are also chronic apologizers. They try to repair with words what they destroy with actions. When I was an entertainment reporter for the *Weekend Today Show,* I was scheduled to attend a screening of an upcoming feature film in preparation for conducting interviews with the film's stars. As is customary, I invited a companion, a guy with whom I had already had one date. Since the doors to such screenings are manned by the very publicists who grant these coveted star interviews, it goes without saying that punctuality is a must.

My date was to pick me up at six-thirty so we could grab a quick bite before the eight o'clock movie. At 6:45 he called and apologized profusely, saying he was stuck at his accountant's office going over some important paperwork. He asked if we could go straight to the movie and have dinner afterward. He sounded sweet and truly sorry, so I consented and he promised to be at my door by seven-thirty.

At seven-thirty he called again, full of apologies and self-deprecating remarks, and assured me he was minutes away. At seven-forty—twenty minutes before the film was to begin— I was fuming. I left a message on his paging voice mail redirecting him to the theater (big mistake on my part!), got in my own car, and tore through West L.A., making it to Beverly Hills in record time. I checked in with the publicist seconds before the movie began. Can you believe that during the movie this guy kept calling my voice mail with apologetic messages that he couldn't find the theater!

Does He Open Doors and Pull Out Chairs Only When It's Called For? Gentlemanly manners are welcome by most women, unless they make us feel inferior.

As "liberated" as I am, as independent as I feel, and as strong as I am perceived, I still like it when a *Homo sapien* larger than I lugs my bags, pulls open heavy doors, and slides a chair under my fanny. However, I have noticed that some men use these traditional rules of gentlemanly behavior to subjugate women. For instance, one man whom I dated for a few months always told me to wait in the passenger seat of the car while he walked *all the way around* his giant SUV to open my door. If I opened it myself before he got there, he criticized me for not knowing how to act like a "lady." I am curious about his definition of the word. Whatever it is, I'm sure it is something *less* than a "man," in his dictionary.

At the other extreme there are men who are earnestly sweet and kind and believe that women should be treated like the goddesses we are. These guys go out of their way with gentlemanly formalities, helping us with our coats, giving us theirs on chilly evenings, pulling out and pushing in chairs, opening all doors, etc. The problem here is that in today's hurried society this can sometimes be downright awkward! My girlfriends tell me they don't want to have to wait at every door for him to catch up if opening it *for him* is more efficient. While the majority of my girlfriends find it always appropriate for a man to open the car door when they're entering his car, it's the exit they take issue with. We certainly don't want to wait like feeble creatures in the passenger seat while men make the twenty-eight-foot trek around the car. An exception might be for a black-tie event or, of course, one's own wedding.

So how do you judge whether a guy is being considerate or condescending with his good graces? It's usually in his attitude. Even an innocuous-sounding line spoken with a smile, like "I wish you'd let me be the man," can speak volumes. This man isn't sure he's a man until you confirm it with your "feminine" (read: submissive) behavior.

On the other hand, if you're the type of woman who eliminates men when they don't act like "the perfect gentleman," then maybe you're the one who is being impractical. In today's world many men are confused about old-fashioned gentlemanly behavior. Some fear that they will offend the more independent of us. Others aren't sure which kind gestures are appropriate and which will earn them a cold glance. So we have to cut them a little slack here. If they at least attempt a few gentlemanly gestures, then they're in the running to be a boyfriend. If they avoid all gentlemanly behaviors, a red light should go off. Ditto if they rush to treat you like a powerless princess.

How Does He Treat the Service Personnel? This is a great indicator of his true personality or at least his personality flaws.

A man who treats waiters and waitresses with disdain has some esteem problems himself. If he sends back his meal, complains about the wine, or speaks in a condescending tone to the server, this guy is a loser. It doesn't matter how wonderfully he talks to you. It doesn't matter if he listens with rapt attention to your stories about your charity work. If he treats other humans with disrespect, he probably doesn't really respect himself. Need more proof? Imagine that you are the waitress and he's speaking to you.

Of course, there are occasions when the food is undercooked, the salad is limp, and the waitress has PMS. In such cases he is certainly allowed to express his displeasure. It's the manner he uses that is important.

Remember, first dates are fantasy nights. He wants to show you he's Prince Charming. He's gotta maintain the reverie not only with you, but with everyone within your earshot and sight line.

What Is His Line of Questioning About You? Is he treating you like a peer, asking about your job and hobbies with genuine interest and attempting to find synergism in your lives?

A man's job on a first date is to sell himself. If he's up for the game, he should be talking about himself, like a peacock showing his feathers, but if his chatter focuses *exclusively* on him, you should be very cautious. Part of a good sales pitch involves demonstrating what you have in common. If it's "all about him," where is there room for you?

So while a man should be selling himself by strutting his stuff, he should also be asking about *you.* He should be asking about your work, your hobbies, your family, your wishes. He should be trying to win you with words. And when you talk, he should be interested in what you have to say. He should listen well. He shouldn't interrupt you. And he should be working to find similarities between your life and his.

In particular, I recommend staying away from one specific kind of trying-to-impress man, who is intent on impressing himself as much as you. I'm talking about the self-centered character who will never be able to truly make room for you in his life—the narcissist.

I mentioned that I had a few romantic run-ins with performer types, and I'll never walk that road again. That is because most of them have adopted the coping mechanism that psychologists call narcissism. This particular personality is not limited to the performing arts, though it runs rampant on most Hollywood sets. You can meet narcissistic CEOs, athletes, chefs, teachers, and even some preachers. What defines narcissism is the desire to be the center of attention.

In simple terms, narcissism is a way that people create the love and adulation that they should have gotten as children and didn't. And generally, the bigger the emotional neglect in infancy and toddlerhood, the bigger the adult narcissist. The biographies of most Hollywood stars illustrate this beautifully, as do the estranged relationships many stars currently have with their parents.

For narcissistic personalities, looking for love means creating it for oneself—with tall tales, plenty of self-compliments, and a supreme interest in one's own life over the lives of others. Essentially they are giving the love to themselves that they haven't gotten from others. It's a very efficient coping strategy, but unfortunately it is only an illusion of love.

It's one I know well, for it guided my own choices for decades. Because I myself am a recovering narcissist, I can spot it miles away. I just listen for the word *I,* which begins the majority of a narcissist's sentences. (Okay, wise girlfriend, please don't do an "I" search throughout this book!)

Think back about your date with "Mr. Me" and ask yourself how much of his trying-to-impress talk wasn't aimed at demonstrating your mutual compatibility, but at convincing you that he is perfect—for any woman. There's a difference between giving you what *he* thinks you want and telling you that it is *he* you should want.

Does He Lie to Impress? Is
he finding too many things in
common with you?

Finding synergism can be one man's enticement and another man's girl-trap. You have to ask yourself if he's telling you the truth or what he thinks you want to hear. Is his excitement for you fitting or is it unbelievable?

Beware the man who tries to find too much in common, whose life seems to mirror yours. Dr. Dory Hollander, author of *101 Lies Men Tell Women,* researched men's lying habits and nearly all the men she interviewed said—without remorse— that they were simply telling women what they wanted to hear.

You may think that your helpful list of target man traits may be under lock and key inside your head, but first dates are hazardous to the security of your inner thoughts. As if by osmosis, that well-thought-out list of yours we talked about in Chapter 3 will be seeping from your head into his, through glances, innuendos, and blatant semantics. On most first dates, a man is trying to uncover your desires so he can fit your wished-for profile (read: He wants to earn your favor so that you'll hit the sheets with him). At the same time, most women are looking for matches to their list. This is a danger-ous game of cat and mouse.

So when he mentions his house in the Hamptons, he sees your eyes open a little wider and knows money is on your list. When he talks about his ski vacation, he sees how quickly you jump to tell him about your favorite ski resorts. Then you outright ask him if he hopes to have a family someday. He nods and smiles like the wolf in Little Red Riding Hood, and by midnight, your feet are in the air.

My advice for first-date interviewing is to ignore all the matches to your list. Instead, look for the *mismatches.* Don't ask him if he's Jewish and then put a check by his name. Ask him what his faith means to him. And if you keep a kosher house, ask him about his house rules. Don't ask him if he's a vegetarian. Ask him what his favorite meal at his favorite restaurant is. Don't ask him if he votes Republican. Ask him who he last voted for and why.

Keep in mind that all men exaggerate on the first few dates. It's part of their call of the wild to impress you. It's a flirting ritual. It's his job to lie—a little. But huge lies are your free pass to the exit door.

And your job is to set the example by being 100 percent honest while keeping personal boundaries intact. You are being completely honest when you say. "I don't feel comfortable enough yet to talk about that with you. When I get to know you better, I'll give you the answer to that question." Of course, you may find that when you get to know him better, he doesn't even deserve an answer to his phone call.

Does He Effortlessly Volunteer Info About His Life?

Does he avoid the hot topics like girlfriends, wives, and children?

This is a more advanced probing than what was possible in the initial phone call. Now you have the added clues of body language and facial expressions to determine if this man is lying. And it's an even better time to decide if this man is hiding something.

It's also a better venue for you to ask more pointed questions. When he's hypnotized by your beauty and sexual appeal, you can catch him off guard with direct questions. My girlfriends are divided on whether to ask a man really personal questions on a first date. I do want to know if he hates his mother, if he has two ex-wives and three estranged children. But I also don't want to scare him off.

After all, if the tables were turned, I don't know how much I'd welcome highly probing personal questions on the first date. On the other hand, I have been asked by many a man on a first date if I like sex, if I enjoy oral sex, and if I have ever participated in a threesome. So what's good for the goose...

I take a gamble. I ask about past (or current) relationships, and I've gotten some interesting answers. I've received some illuminating responses that run the gamut from surprisingly honest tales of too many serial relationships to stone silence at the mention of a possible wife.

We are a culture of what anthropologists call perceived

monogamy. Some scientists, like biologist Judy Stamps, speculate that we are actually in transition from a polygamous society (multiple sexual partners over the course of a lifetime) to a monogamous one (one man, one woman for the long term). That's good news for women, who tend to be slightly more monogamous than men, and best news of all for children, who can fare better with the input of both parents.

But here's our dilemma. If a man is actively pursuing you, he's probably got some hearty levels of testosterone flowing through his body, and he may be a primate in transition from plural partners to singular. (Read: There's a chance he could have a wife and kids. Or at least a girlfriend or fiancée.)

So it's a good idea to ask about them. And listen closely to what he says. For example, I have had many a first date with guys who trashed their exes so badly, I pictured my own name inserted after each disparaging adjective. Scary stuff. One guy, a brain surgeon who obviously knew little about the organ he routinely sliced into, even told me the nickname of his ex was psycho-Suzy! Fast-forward to our breakup: Wacko-Wendy is not the kind of press I wanted. It wasn't worth taking the risk of discovering if ole Suzy was truly a candidate for the psych ward. I moved on.

I believe that the sooner you get the truth or let him tell the lies you can bust him on, the sooner you'll be on your way toward a better boyfriend. So *ask him about his relationships.*

Does He Take Complete Control of the Evening or Present You with Options?

From food selection to a great dessert place to an after-dinner movie, do you have a voice?

Yes, it's great to be wined and dined at some fantastic unfamiliar place. And it's sometimes great to have a spontaneous guy who is full of surprises. But it's also nice to have at least some small say in things. I mentioned earlier that we like men to have a plan, but once that plan is under execution, we also like men to have a little flexibility, and some consideration for our preferences. After all, you are not a prop in his fantasy. He should be attempting to create *your* fantasy as a way to win your love.

One high-powered theatrical agent whom I had just one date with insisted that he take me to a music store after dinner. He had discussed music over the meal and stated that even though he hadn't seen my CD collection, he felt it was lacking in certain classics, namely the Beatles, the Rolling Stones, and Eric Clapton. I actually thought he was joking until he turned his BMW into the Tower Records parking lot. Then he hastily escorted me through the store's aisles, shoving CDs in my arms along the way. Was I burned when I ended up at the cash register with ten pricey CDs—and he suddenly disappeared!

So if, at the end of dinner, he commands that the cigar bar of his choice or the bakery around the corner is definitely next, and not up for discussion, then he loses points on the cooperative front. Romantic pairing in the human species takes enormous cooperation because the business of child rearing is lengthy and labor intensive. If this guy is not showing flexibility and a willingness to step aside on some rulings, then he will certainly be a miserable family man and probably a bad boyfriend.

QUESTION #9

Does He Allow You to Pick Up or Split the Check? Either he thinks you're not worth impressing or he's a gigolo.

The money clue is critical on a first date. It's something, I might add, that took me ages to understand. There is one rule and one rule only on a first date: He pays in full. Don't even offer to pick up the tip, the parking, or his subway token. This man is trying to awe you. He is wired unconsciously to compete for resources and display resources when attempting to mate. It's basic science. And if he deviates from this behavior, he has some screws loose. Don't wait around to find out which ones.

Case in point. I was once fixed up on a blind date with a handsome feature-film director of photography. Since he fitted my projected boyfriend profile of being artistic while having a serious career, I was excited to meet him. On top of that, he turned out to be tall!

Now, this was no average blind date, because the couple who created the fix-up wanted to accompany us to dinner. Can you say "uncomfortable evening"? Our interaction was limited to stolen glances while trying to keep up with the superfluous chatter led by the other couple.

When the check finally arrived, my date revealed himself and I missed the red flag. When the other man quickly took the check and placed his credit card on top of it, I was ready for the usual male haggling over who would "get" to pay the check. But it never came. My date didn't so much as offer to split the check with the other guy. I made a mental note but excused him because he was cute and seemed relatively smart. There had to be a good reason for this.

Date number two was scheduled during date number one. Because Academy Award night was one week away and because I just happened to have remodeled my home, complete with a thirty-five-inch television, it was not so gently suggested that I host this foursome again. With some pasta in my belly and the vino clouding my judgment, I readily consented.

Date number two: I spent two hundred dollars at various epicurean shops attempting to pull off an elaborate Martha Stewart routine. My gorgeous date showed up empty-handed. No wine. No flowers. And still I missed the clue. I ended the evening with some kisses on my bed but got him out the door with all clothes still buttoned.

Date number three: We were on our own. Our first solo flight since dumping Mr. and Mrs. Roper. I was ecstatic. He suggested dinner Friday night sometime after his shoot wrapped. He called at six P.M. to alert me that he'd probably finish by eight-thirty. I asked him if he'd like me to make a dinner reservation. He said yes, thank you. He felt like having seafood. Then he asked a question that made my heart break. He said, "Can you pick up this one because I'm really short of cash?"

I caught my breath and found enough words to express my displeasure with the idea. He told me not to worry about it. He'd find the money somewhere. He did. He paid for that dinner, but we never went out again. I still don't know how a thirty-five-year-old man who works on major motion pictures can't afford to impress a woman with one night out.

The lesson here is that I should probably not have gone out with him after date number one. And, for sure, I shouldn't have paid for date number two. I would have saved myself two weeks of heart-pulsating yearning and a huge letdown.

P.S. He called a year or so later (I was in a relationship) to apologize.

Does He Give You Grief Over a Simple Hug or Good-Night Peck? This is an old-fashioned rule but has stood the test of time: You are in charge of the pace of physical contact.

It's sophomoric for a guy to pressure a woman for any sexual act, even a kiss on the lips. This is not high school. And this is not the free-sex seventies. This is the millennium, with herpes, hepatitis, and AIDS.

Having said that, you must remember that you are on a date with a M-A-N, the animal whose behavior is often ruled by testosterone. You can't fault him for *trying* to go further than you'd like to. After all, you are a babe. But you can eliminate him big time if he attempts more than once. If you stop his hand on your leg, turn your mouth away from his tongue, or wiggle away from his embrace, you are communicating an important message to him.

Now, since many men convicted of date rape say they felt that the woman's early rejections were part of the foreplay, you should also issue a very clear, vocal "NO." You can do it with a smile, but it must be stated out loud.

And I mention your rejections of sexual advances on the first date for a good reason: Don't ever *accept* those advances on a first date. If you think for one minute that you are in a trusting bond with a man after a few hours together, you are being completely disillusioned. Trading sex for intimacy just doesn't work. And after interviewing many, many girlfriends, I can confidently say that first-date sex rarely helps a relationship sustain itself. More often it shortens it. Why sign on the line before you've even seen the details in the contract?

Okay, girlfriends. Get your pencils out for the first-date score sheet.

First-Date
Score Sheet Report Card

Note: Each boyfriend candidate starts out with a new rating of 50. From there his behavior either earns or loses him points.

1 Is he a stickler about transportation?

_____ Offered to pick you up (+5)

_____ Didn't mind when you preferred to drive (+5)

_____ Wouldn't let you bring your own car (–15)

_____ Expected you to meet him somewhere (–20)

_____ Expected you to pick him up! (–30)

2 Does he veer from his ETA?

_____ He's an early bird. (–10)

_____ He's on time—exactly. (–5)

_____ He's five minutes late. (+10)

_____ He's six to fifteen minutes late. (–10)

_____ He's later than fifteen minutes and calls from a cell phone with excuses. (–20)

_____ He's later than fifteen minutes and doesn't call with apologies. (–35)

3 Does he open doors and pull out chairs only when it's called for?

_____ Opened car door when you got in (+2)

_____ Opened car door when you got out (+2)

_____ Opened door to restaurant, museum, stadium, etc. (+2)

_____ Ordered for you in the restaurant after asking what you want (+2)

_____ Helped you on with your coat (+2)
_____ All of the above (–10)
_____ None of the above (–20)

4 How does he treat the service personnel?

Give him a rating of one to ten on how
courteous he was with the server, usher,
ticket agent, valet parker, etc. (1–10)
*Now subtract four points if he did any of the
following:*
_____ Sent an item back to the kitchen (–4)
_____ Complained to you that the service
was bad (–4)
_____ Complained to the establishment that
the service was bad (–4)
_____ Tipped poorly (yes, glance at his credit-
card receipt as he signs it!) (–4)

5 What is his line of questioning about you?

_____ He asked about your job. (+2)
_____ He asked about your hobbies. (+2)
_____ He asked about your family. (+2)
_____ He asked about your past relationships
in a nonjudging way. (+2)
_____ He asked very little about you. (–20)
_____ He asks nothing about you except
where you like to eat or dance. (–20)

6 Does he lie to impress?

_____ You left the date feeling that you have
an unlikely number of things in
common. (–10)
_____ He seemed to exaggerate a bit. (0)
_____ He told you something that you know
is an obvious lie. (–25)

7 **Does he effortlessly volunteer information about his life?**

_____ Talked about his past relationships with ease (+5)

_____ Spoke disparagingly about his exes (–30)

_____ You felt he withheld some information. (–20)

_____ Was defensive about such questions (–40)

8 **Does he take complete control of the evening?**

_____ He asked you to participate in date options. (+5)

_____ He went with one of your suggestions. (+5)

_____ He turned down your idea. (–10)

_____ He didn't ask for your input at all. (–20)

9 **Does he allow you to pick up or split the check?**

_____ He paid for _everything_. (+10)

_____ He paid for everything except incidentals (e.g., parking, valet tip). (+5)

_____ He suggested you split the check. (–50)

_____ He asked you to pay it all. (–70)

10 **Does he give you grief over a simple hug or good-night peck?**

_____ He tried to get more. (–5)

_____ He tried more than once. (–15)

_____ He placed his hand on your butt, upper thigh, breast without asking first. (–50)

_____ He made a negative comment about you "not giving more." (−20)

_____ He was a perfect gentleman and graciously accepted your chosen good-night gesture. (+10)

GRADING THE FIRST-DATE TEST

Note: To calculate this grade so far, add up the scores from the Meet and Greet, the Telephone Test, and the First-Date Test, then divide by three.

The candidate must score at least an average of B+ to proceed with you any further.

- **Exceptional (90–100) A+**

- **Excellent (80–89) A**

- **Very Good (75–79) B+**

- **Good (70–74) B**

- **Satisfactory (65–69) C+**

- **Minimum Pass (60–64) C**

- **Failure (50–59) D**

- **Complete Failure (0–49) F**

the five-date consistency test

> Eventually you will catch on to the frog who pretends to be a prince, because the one thing he truly can't make over is who he really is. The question is never whether you'll catch on, only when.
>
> —Dr. Dory Hollander,
> *101 Lies Men Tell Women*

Now the test gets really tough. You've had at least one stimulating phone conversation, you've squirmed like a schoolgirl through a wonderful dinner, and now he thinks you're hooked. Maybe you are.

For that reason it's crucial that you work hard to refrain from using rationalizations about his negative behavior should it peek out from under his princely veneer. During the next few dates, guys will still be on their best behavior, so you have to look for subtle clues about their emotional maturity and compassion quotient. It's time to watch him relax a little and reveal some of his true self.

First of all, don't despair if your man tells you he'll call and then appears to have forgotten that Alexander Graham Bell ever graced the planet. All men end every date by saying "I'll call you." It's no different from us saying "See ya" to the last waiter who served us. We probably won't. And we'd think he was pretty strange if he took us literally and looked for us every night at the same table.

One of the hardest parts of the mating game for the female competitor is wondering if a man will call us back. Consciously, of course, we get anxious because we aren't sure if he will. But subconsciously, we know whether the date went well or not, and deep down we know if he is as interested as we are. We know if there is a match and a budding trust.

My advice during the waiting period: Focus on your life. Continue to live your girlfriend-tested life as if the date were a singular event with no follow-up. When he does call again, you need not be surprised, jubilant, or relieved, but simply satisfied that this is what is meant to be.

If the date went well, it is subconsciously understood that he will call. But if he doesn't call, work hard to abate your anxiety with stress-reducing activities. Exercise, meditate, stay busy, and believe that the best outcome is happening. Do you really want to be with someone who doesn't want to be with you? Will you like yourself more just because you can motivate this or any guy to pursue you? You are a goddess. You are a giant ovum poised to take applications from speedy sperm. If there is a mutant sperm who has lost sight of his mission or who is fragmented with too many ovum to attack, then he is a reject.

Assuming he does call, this postdate communication should be treated not unlike his first phone call—the rules stay the same—except you now should have more subjects to browse after your rousing first-date discourse.

You may receive a couple of calls before the next date as the two of you coordinate your schedules and use the phone to get to know each other better (in some cases you might begin trading e-mail messages as well). But a certain formality is still required. If he's already using too much sexually suggestive talk, or flattering you too much, then his objective is not to be good boyfriend, but a good lay.

In addition to the original telephone rules that I've outlined, as the second date becomes the third, and in time the fifth is on the horizon, be aware of his usage of communication tools.

One last reminder: During this sensitive getting-to-know-each-other phase, it's important to consider that you may also be taking *his* test. That doesn't mean you should alter your behavior to meet his expectations, but it does mean you have to watch for clues that he's ready to move on. Most men don't break up. When the majority of men want out of a relationship, they simply behave badly until you get weary of the antics and do the breaking up yourself. A good chunk of the male population aren't even sure they want you to break up with them. These guys would prefer to put out little effort while you hang around as a sex toy and they continue to shop for Mrs. Right. I've had this conversation with men and I know it's true. The questions in the next two chapters are as much a test of his potential as they are a test of your ability to get the messages he may be sending to you.

QUESTION #1

Does He Play Phone Tag? He knows where and when to call you, yet you always seem to end up being "it."

The phone tag guys used to drive me nuts. I would come home and always seemed to have "just missed" their call. I felt bad that I was never at my office when they called, and not home either. Then I got a pager and gave the number to my latest heartthrob irritant. And he still called at home when I wasn't there!

It was then that I realized that this man didn't really want to talk to me. He just wanted to do his duty and check in, or maybe keep me hanging on a line while he was still shopping for a bigger fish. It made me crazy, so I busted him on it. Of course, he denied his behavior. Perhaps he wasn't aware he was doing it. At any rate, after the practice continued for a while, I dumped him.

As I've said, most men do not have the balls to break up with a woman or tell her they don't want to see her again. This is most true when they have little invested in the relationship. Most men would rather volunteer for the draft than whisper honest oral utterances to a woman. Instead, they do one of three things: (a) They take a long time to return calls, (b) they stop calling altogether, or (c) they call when they know they won't get you.

We are in a post–technological revolution era. There is no need to have communication problems. You can have a phone at work, at home, in your car, in your purse, or you can keep a pager on your belt, and most important, you can communicate to him when you will be available to take calls so that if he really wants to talk to you, he'll find you.

As an excellent girlfriend candidate, you must also avoid pulling him into silly communication games. Tell him where you'll be and when, and then let him hang himself by not calling. If he does play games, walk away.

On the other side of the coin, there are guys who start a daily telephone check-in after just one date. Again, these are the trying-too-hard types who have to be nixed because they

have esteem issues or poor impulse control, both problems
that they must deal with before entering your life.

How Does He Use E-mail? Is he trying to reveal his inner self through the written word, or distance himself from you?

E-mail is a strange and wonderful thing. First of all, it's highly
personal and, even in a business setting, quite informal. You
can avoid receptionists and voice mail and instantly get into
someone's head. The written word can be very seductive. People tend to be more honest when they don't have to monitor
their voice and the fear of confrontation is eliminated. (I've
used e-mail a couple of times to execute my anger because I
knew I'd chicken out in person.)

But as candid as e-mail is, it is also a creator of space. It's
an easy way to distance yourself from someone you don't want
to get too close to. If you suspect that your boyfriend candidate might be using e-mail this way, and the e-mail "tag" is
going on for too long, simply ask him to telephone you. If
he doesn't, then he doesn't really want to talk to you, or see
you...unless it's convenient for his social schedule. Again, if
this is true, it's time for you to move on.

Is He Still Making and Consistently Keeping Plans? This is still the court-ship phase and he should remain the gentleman.

One good date does not a boyfriend make. If he's to pass this test, he'd better be prepared to court you for a while. And you'd better be prepared to let him. Don't start offering to make reservations or pick up checks. And don't be satisfied with dates that consist of just "hanging out" at his place or yours.

Remember you are a catch, and he is a mere mortal trying to win your favor. Not that the ensuing dates must all be formal and expensive. They can certainly be casual and cheap. But they have to be initiated by him, approved by you, and designed to facilitate a growing bond.

I once went out with a music industry executive who thought he had done his duty with only two dates—a movie and dessert came first, followed the next week by a romantic oceanside dinner and moonlight beach walk. After that, he mostly suggested that I drive to his house to have dinner in his neighborhood (I often consented because his neighborhood is Malibu, a far better locale for weekend retreats than my humble Brentwood apartment was), and usually I'd arrive while he was still in the throes of a workout or basketball game. Then I'd sit and wait while he showered, and finally he'd saunter downstairs and ask, "So do we have to go out or can we order in?"

Based on the poor judgment detailed in my relationship history in the rest of this book, you can probably ascertain the punch line to this story. I stayed with the guy for six months and he turned out to be a bit of an agoraphobic, not to mention a philanderer—it seems I wasn't the only one willing to make that trek to Malibu. Ironically, during our "breakup," it was he who uttered, "I wish you'd let me court you more." That statement told me very clearly that I was too cooperative, so he got lazy.

We're looking for consistency here, girlfriends. We're looking for a guy to go the extra mile. In a real relationship there are all kinds of occasions when the man must carry the burden for a while, so it's important that we determine whether or not he's capable of this.

I know one young couple with a new baby. He's an attorney and she's in law school. When her final exams roll around, this guy becomes a full-time Mr. Mom, even taking time away from the office to care for the little one. I know another couple where the woman was bedridden for months during a high-risk pregnancy, and through it all, her husband did everything, running the house like a blue-chip corporation. I also know someone who had breast cancer (she has since passed away) whose significant other couldn't handle the pressure, and while she attended a macrobiotic cooking course, he blew their savings on heroin. I'd venture to wager that this man probably never planned and paid for five full dates when he and his partner first got together.

If he can't be at the helm for five dates while he's attempting to be on his best behavior, then how will he perform when the chips are down for real and you're unable to help?

Has He Followed Up on the "Little Promises" He's Made? Whether it's to fix your car stereo or make a business referral call on your behalf, he must consistently keep his promises.

Single women need men for all kinds of things. If you're a special woman who knows how to do an oil change on your car, replace the flapper on your incessantly running toilet, and connect the gas hose to your new dryer, then good for you. But for the rest of us, there remain a myriad of tasks, be they messy, heavy, or tedious, that are just better done by someone with hair on his chest. Of course, we know we are independent and can *hire* a man to do all of these things (sometimes that's a great way to meet a good one!), but it's so much fun once in a while to play damsel in distress and watch them run to help.

And I ask you, who better to help than an incoming boyfriend? Realistically, possible boyfriends may be the *only* ones who run to your aid. Entrenched boyfriends are often too complacent, and outgoing ones are too disgruntled. Use their sexual energy wisely, and while you're doing it, test them on their reliability.

Most important to watch for are the promises themselves. Are they suggesting ways that they can enhance your life? And are they then following through on those promises?

When I purchased my first home, there seemed to be a million little fixes required before it would become my very own palace. Fortunately, I was dating at the time and was surprised to learn that modern men have talents over and above the art of hitting a keyboard and remote control.

Over the course of a few months, the current beau lifted boxes, assembled furniture, hung heavy pictures and mirrors, put a purifier on my water line, and—my favorite—installed dimmer switches everywhere.

For some reason, this is always an easy part of the test for me. I think it's because my father and my brothers were all handy around the house. If I needed a shelf for my books, I just said the word and someone built me one.

When a man lets me down by not following through on these kind of promises, it definitely doesn't jibe with what my early programming taught me, so I have no problem deeming him to be useless. I know that this is a huge indicator of his future reliability, and I also know that energy in this area declines as couplehood closes in. Therefore I dump him early on if he lets me down in this department.

Beware: There's another breed of animal who knows how much you'll love this kind of attention. This people-pleaser volunteers too much and uses his helpful tasks as ways to get to see you more often. Slow this loser down. He's going way too fast, too soon, and needs to have some boundaries of his own.

Has He Displayed Any Anger? Any signs of uncontrolled agitation at this stage could signal an anger-management problem.

Anger is an important emotion. It tells us that something isn't right. It tells us that someone has stepped across one of our boundaries. It tells us to make a different choice.

It's important that we recognize anger in ourselves and find a healthy outlet through which to execute it. Bottled-up anger can be as dangerous as anger inappropriately vented. For me, writing this book became a kind of anger therapy. Describing all my past social violations helped me come to terms with my anger and, as I mentioned earlier, helped me become more clear about my boundaries. I also write letters about my feelings, or write about them in a journal. A good cry in a warm tub is another welcome outlet for me.

Unfortunately, most men in our culture do not possess the tools of anger management that women do. Open displays of anger are regarded as "unfeminine," so we have quiet ways of expressing it. Women do, however, have permission (and are even expected) to show other emotions. Men, on the other hand, are told that anger is quite masculine. On the playing field, the mantra is "Fight! Fight! Fight!" Anger is accepted, but the underlying emotion, hurt feelings, is not. When they are violated, they are told to "suck it up" and that "big boys don't cry."

As adults, when men get hurt, many "suck it up" until it becomes uncontainable and then they burst—with the only emotion they know—anger. Or some constantly display it physically, by using a loud voice, throwing objects, or, worst of all, throwing humans. Interestingly enough, recent studies on anger show that when anger is expressed physically it doesn't act as a release but instead serves to exacerbate the emotion and its ensuing physiological responses—increased heart rate and blood pressure.

I have a theory that television sports can have a cathartic effect by allowing men a safe place to "feel" their anger. In the same way that you and I use a tearjerker movie to tap into our feminine angst, men use sports to symbolically "act out" aggression—aggression that was a necessary part of our species' survival for millions of years. It's as if they have a hunter/protector gene that is out of place in our modern culture.

(By the way, my theory is only that. There are feminist groups that would disagree with me by using the statistic that incidents of domestic violence increase on Super Bowl Sunday. Personally, I think that has more to do with alcohol consumption than with the game.)

So if anger is a natural and healthy emotion, how much should we accept when it's displayed to us? Do we break up with every boyfriend who gets mad? No. However, I can positively say that during the first five dates you should put up with no anger at all.

I once stood at an airport ticket counter on about date number five (why was I flying to Florida with this man so early in our courtship?), and the man I was with got into a fight with the ticket agent over seat selection. I mean, it was a screaming I-want-the-name-of-your-superior kind of fight. I was so embarrassed. Later on, this guy turned out to be an insecure man who huffed and puffed at anyone he thought was weaker than him—and I think he thought it would impress me!

I'll say it again, and you'll probably hear it one more time: Men should be trying to astonish you. They should be on their best behavior for a good long time. This is the courting phase. If anger cannot be controlled during this crucial testing period, then you have to wonder how much control a man will have when he feels comfortable with you.

There's another kind of anger, the passive-aggressive kind, which you should also be conscious of. This kind of anger takes the form of constant subtle complaining (not always directed at you), long silences, and subversive behaviors that indicate a disrespect for your wishes. It may be a signal that this man is unhappy in the relationship, or unhappy in general. His moods should be fairly consistent for a time. If he starts to whine about everything wrong with his life, he may be whining about you. Remember, most guys don't break up, and they often don't get more cheerful than what you're seeing now if they're exhibiting sorrow signs. Dump him now.

Has He Begun to Introduce You to His Friends?

If you've spent five full dates alone, you should wonder if you're intended to be his private sex slave, or if he has any friends at all.

Relationships do not exist in a vacuum. They exist in our culture. Dating is part of the intricate set of experiences called a life. If he hasn't been introducing you to his, you should wonder why.

It is not required by date number five that you meet his parents and any offspring he may have. Close family might only be exposed to you when he's sure you'll be in his life longer than one football season. But you should have met at least one or two of his friends.

The reason is this: If he's interested in you as relationship material, he'll want some input from some of his peers. C'mon, admit it. You do the same thing. Your girlfriends' opinions often help you form your own. So if he's not doing this, why not? Is his life not worth revealing to you? Could it be an embarrassment? Or what about you? Is he hiding you from the people who might tell his *girlfriend?*

What Are You Learning About the Length of His Past Relationships? Now the truth can be told, and the skeletons should be filing out of the closet.

You might have given him a break if, on the first date, he evaded questions about his relationship history, because he may still have accumulated enough points to move on with you. Back then he was doing his best to appear as your fantasy man. But now the truth should be coming out, and the length of his past commitments is one of the biggest determining factors of his long-term potential.

If the man is over twenty-five, he should have had at least one long-term relationship under his belt. I define long term as around three years or more. It's long enough to have lasted through one early life stage, high school, college, or a first job. When we are young, life evolves at an accelerated pace while we're trying to define ourselves. We change schools. We change jobs. We change friends. And we change romantic partners, all as we move from phase to phase. But one three-year relationship should have happened by the age of twenty-five.

If he's near forty and hasn't had at least one (or two!) relationships of at least four years, there is a good chance he is a commitment-phobic.

On the other hand, if he has one failed marriage behind him, this may not be a bad thing. He at least knows of the enormous compromise that comes with marriage and is probably shell-shocked from a stint in divorce court (the division of assets, child custody, alimony, nasty attorneys, etc.). A man with this kind of life experience will probably be more choosy next time around and respect the value of a good relationship.

But if he has been turning over romantic partners at breakneck speed, then you must be concerned about his ability to truly become intimate with anyone. And if a man with this history is over thirty-five and has never been near a therapist's office, then run. Fast.

I once had dinner with a thirty-four-year-old man who told me his longest relationship up to that point had been nine months. In almost two decades of girl-chasing, this man hadn't committed himself to one calendar year! We became platonic friends rather than romantic partners.

But a high number of short relationships isn't the only red flag from his past you should be aware of. Another guy I knew was thirty-nine and had three lengthy periods (like years!) of celibacy on his relationship résumé.

Both of these men have intimacy issues that must be addressed. There are two ways to avoid human intimacy: to not stay long enough or stay away altogether. Your boyfriend candidate should employ neither of these behaviors.

Does He Continue to Show Earnest Interest in Your Life? That includes friends, jobs, and passions, other than bedroom sports.

Any guy can get through one or two dates appearing interested in more than your Victoria Secret collection. Only a few guys can get through five dates sporting a veneer of curiosity in something they're not really interested in.

One way to tell his true interest level is to test his memory banks. Does he remember the details of that recent fender bender that had you so bummed? Does he remember how many siblings you told him you have? How about your boss's name, or your favorite foods? Note: He will always recall your age and bra size, so information like this doesn't count.

I know the challenge of being a player because, for a time, I was a bit of a player-chick myself (read: afraid of real intimacy, so I watered down the milk with a bunch of less-than-appropriate mates). My roommate and I used to joke that we couldn't date more than four men at once because at number five we would start to get the stories confused. I remember once getting a blank stare from a man after I asked the location of the BCBG franchise that he had told me his sister owned. Oops! Wrong guy, no sister.

So if he's mixing up stories and attributing another woman's past to you, don't dismiss it as an honest mistake. If he really wanted to remember, he could. I bet most men can remember the entire NBA playoff schedule.

Next, check his empathy pulse. When you reveal any personal problems/dilemmas, what is his reaction? I once spent ten minutes on the phone telling a guy I was dating that my boss was an egotistical tyrant who regarded me as a visual object rather than an intellectual creature, and he responded with, "Cool. Hey, guess who's on Letterman tonight?"

QUESTION #9

Does He Call You Baby, Hon, or Sweetie? It is much too early for terms of endearment!

Sweet pet names are common in all relationships, but if you have just begun dating this guy, you are not yet in a relationship!

Terms of endearment at this stage exhibit an immature level of familiarity. He's trying to make it seem as if you're closer than you really are. He's feigning intimacy in hopes that you'll fall for it. He wants you to mistake his loving name for you for love itself. Of course, it isn't love, and it's not even a clear promise of love, so he knows he'll be able to get out of it later if he needs to.

Besides, it should make you feel more like a number than a specialty. I was once passionately kissing a guy at the end of date number four (we hadn't hit the sack yet) and he whispered, "Oh, b-a-b-y." I suddenly had the feeling that this form of address rolled off his tongue way too easily and wondered if perhaps he had forgotten my name. Later, when I learned of his Don Juan bent, I became convinced it had been his way to keep the names straight once the blood poured from his brain to his penis.

Sex! Is It Kind, Loving, and Complete with Foreplay and After-Play? Expect him to get the warm towel to clean up, cuddle you for as long as you need, and sleep on the wet spot!

It's especially difficult to test him at this stage if his signals are drowned out by the wails of your orgasms. But I know that the flesh is weak and our culture lenient, so there's a good chance you've slept with him by now. (Hurrah for your discipline if you haven't!)

So a lesson in sex is probably appropriate at this point in the exam. Long-term boyfriends might sometimes roll over and grab the remote after an orgasm, but boyfriend candidates are trying to earn your love. If sex is not perfectly loving, gentlemanly, and considerate, then this man is disrespecting you. Do not allow it.

Down the road sex can be kinky. Sex can be brief. Sex can be one-sided in terms of giving. Sex can be a lot of things in the safety of trusting monogamy. But "dating sex" is different.

Dating sex is cordial. Dating sex is about mutual pleasure. Dating sex involves long conversations while you're snuggled under the covers in the dewy afterglow of orgasm. Dating sex involves frank but respectful talk about personal preferences, birth control, and sexually transmitted diseases *before* hitting the sack.

I remember one man with a hard-on pressing in against me while we hugged in the back of a restaurant/bar, and at the same time vehemently stating that he "did *not* want to talk about AIDS." Sorry, pal, no discourse, no intercourse.

And on that subject, *he* should come equipped with latex condoms and so should you. Don't settle for the risky lamb-skin variety and his whining that he can't feel anything through latex. Dating sex is all about latex.

If you've followed the statistics on females' being infected with the AIDS virus, you know that unprotected sex is more risky for us than it is for men. We're the ones who accept deposits. So a boyfriend candidate will also understand when you tell him about your no-blow-job policy until both of you have been tested. If he puts up more than a tiny fuss, this guy is immature.

He'll also understand if you choose not to go "all the way." He may express disappointment, but he will also be understanding of your reasoning. You are at the controls. This is your body, your domain, your kingdom, and you, as the queen, can decide who enters, by which gate, and how far into your court he'll be allowed.

Now test him again with the following score sheet.

Five-Date
Score Sheet Report Card

Note: This boyfriend candidate starts out with a new rating of 50. From there his behavior either earns or loses him points.

1 Does he play phone tag?

____ Called once since the date and you were home (0)

____ Called. Left message. Didn't call back at the time you requested. (−10)

____ Called. You exchanged messages and he called back when you suggested. (+10)

____ Called twice and missed even though you told him where you'd be (−20)

____ Called too many times on too many of your phones (−15)

2 How does he use e-mail?

____ He's opening up like a book but doesn't call. (+5)

____ He writes deep e-mails and calls sometimes, too. (+10)

____ He leaves short, to-the-point messages but doesn't call. (−10)

____ He takes more than two days to answer your e-mails. (−10)

____ He's not on-line. (0)

3 **Is he still making and consistently keeping plans?**

____ Planned and initiated all five dates (+10)

____ Planned and initiated four dates (0)

____ Planned and initiated only three dates (−10)

____ Planned and initiated only the first two dates (−15)

____ Planned and initiated only the first date (−20)

4 **Has he followed up on the "little promises" he's made?**

____ Made no promises to enhance your life in small ways (−10)

____ Made a bunch of promises and followed up on none (−20)

____ Made a couple of promises and came through on one but not the other (+5)

____ Made a couple of promises and followed through on both (+15)

____ Made a lot of promises and followed through on them all (−10)

5 **Has he displayed any anger?**

____ Yes (−30)

____ No (+15)

6 **Has he begun to introduce you to his friends?**

____ Yes, one friend (+10)

____ No, a few friends (+15)

____ No, none at all (−20)

____ Yes, friends, family, and/or coworkers (0)

7 **What are you learning about the length of his past relationships?**

---- No relationships that lasted more than three years (−15)

---- One or two long relationships (+10)

---- Seems to mention many, many ex-girlfriends (−30)

8 **Does he continue to show earnest interest in your life?**

---- Forgot one important factor about you that you had told him (−−10)

---- Confused more than one story (−20)

---- Seems to be following all your life dramas (+10)

9 **Does he call you baby, hon, or sweetie?**

---- Once, in the heat of passion (−5)

---- A few times (−10)

---- Seems to have forgotten your name (−25)

---- Only calls you by your name (+10)

10 **Is the sex loving and kind?**

---- He asked you to do an act you feel is way too personal for getting-to-know-each-other sex. (−5)

---- He talks too dirty too early. (−5)

---- He grabbed the remote too soon after his climax (he forgot the after-play cuddle). (−5)

---- Sex is too quick. (−5)

---- He complains or tries to pressure you into doing more than you're ready for. (−5)

_____ He doesn't have a condom with him.
(−10)

_____ He is comfortable talking about AIDS.
(+5)

_____ He is comfortable talking about birth
control. (+5)

_____ He doesn't complain after you've
stated your ground rules. (+5)

_____ His after-play was great—he cleaned
up and cuddled and _talked_! (+10)

_____ You haven't slept together yet. (+15)

GRADING THE FIVE-DATE TEST

Note: This grade is calculated by adding the scores
from the Meet and Greet, the Telephone Test, the
First-Date Test, and the Five-Date Test, then dividing
by four.

The candidate must score at least an average
of A to proceed with you any further.

■ **Exceptional (90–100) A+**

■ **Excellent (80–89) A**

■ **Very Good (75–79) B+**

■ **Good (70–74) B**

■ **Satisfactory (65–69) C+**

■ **Minimum Pass (60–64) C**

■ **Failure (50–59) D**

■ **Complete Failure (0–49) F**

the ninety-day probation test

> "If this be obsession deliver me
> A passing infatuation, deliver me
> A feeling lacking in purity deliver
> me"
>
> —Tracy Chapman,
>   from the album *Telling Stories*

Is it time to promote this candidate? By the end of ninety days, you should be a couple. Three months of dating is sufficient time to determine if monogamy is suitable to both of you.

For those of you who are used to immature relationships, here's a reality check—talking twice a week and having sex on Saturdays does not a couple make. If the relationship hasn't advanced to the point where you're having honest conversations about exclusivity, monogamy, and indeed a quasi love, then dump him now. He's not ready for anything intimate yet.

Here is the fifth part of the test, ten questions that determine if this is a relationship now that he's becoming himself.

QUESTION #1

Do His Acquaintances Call You by Name? These are innocuous people. It shouldn't hurt if they know he has a girlfriend.

We all have a circle of tertiary acquaintances whom we are legislated to be friendly with—our bank teller, our office receptionist, our mail carrier, our building maintenance person, the gardener, the cop on the corner, the guy who changes the oil in our car, etc. Often these are people we can "try out" a boyfriend with. Not that their opinions matter, but it is a way for us to gauge our own feelings about the relationship by introducing our new beau. It's a small risk for a man to introduce you by name to the woman who fluffs his latté every morning, but it can help *him* get ready to introduce you to the world. After all, this is the first step into his world.

These people can sometimes even—if you're really lucky—

give you some insight into his character. Watch how they regard him. Do they really seem to like and respect him or are they only formally cordial? I was once given a clear red-light warning when I entered a new beau's apartment accompanied by him. He introduced me to his concierge, a woman. After smiling and handing him his deliveries, she made a "joke" about his character. "Girlfriend," she laughingly said, "let me tell you about this man!" By the tone of her mischievous giggle, the news was not good. She wasn't able to say anything else because he quickly scooted me into the elevator. But she didn't have to. Thank you, girlfriend, wherever you are! I shall always be indebted to you.

The people who work around his home or office should be used to seeing you, and he may even have offhandedly mentioned you, if not introduced you. By the way, if your boyfriend candidate ignores all these people and doesn't even have a friendly though distant relationship with them, you should wonder whether he's a bit of a classist.

One other sidebar: If these people include personal assistants, managers, publicists, agents, or Secret Service men, know that their primary function is to be gatekeepers for your man. They may appear friendly to you, but they'll close the door on you in an instant if he says the word, so don't count these people as passive indicators of his willingness to let you into his life.

It is a good sign, however, if he's sending you to the guy who always installs his car stereos, or the woman who does all his tailoring. The man who is afraid of commitment will keep these people secret so that he can have a "clean" life when things don't work out with you. The man who optimistically sees potential in your relationship, and who has self-confidence, won't shrink at the idea of seeing you at his dry cleaners should you break up.

Where Does He Keep Your Toothbrush or Photo? If the trails you leave behind are all neatly swept under the rug, this man may be avoiding commitment.

We all leave "stuff" behind in romantic relationships. I think it's our metaphorical way of peeing on a fire hydrant or marking our spot. We mostly do it unconsciously. Perhaps it's our brain telling us we'll have to (get to!) see him at least one more time if it's to pick up that sweater we left behind.

In fact, I have quite consciously used the tactic when I suspected a man was cheating on me. I deliberately would leave a hairpin, a lipstick, or my favorite, a tampon, in some nook or cranny of his bathroom where a woman might find it. I know this works, because one boyfriend called and *got mad at me(!)* because a woman found my hair scrunchy in his bathroom drawer.

Aside from using trails as a war tactic, they can also be a sweet symbol indicating that both your lives are merging. He sticks your photo up somewhere. You clear a small space in your makeup drawer for his shaving cream. He buys a few extra hangers. And you make room amongst your *Cosmopolitan* magazines for issues of *Popular Mechanics, Motor Trend,* or *Sports Illustrated.*

This is a logical first step into couplehood. If this is not happening—and you are sleeping with the man—then it might be time for coitus interruptus!

Does He Always Reserve Saturday Nights for You?
Look it up in the dictionary. The definition of Saturday night is "couples night."

You shouldn't have to check his weekend schedule after three months of dating. He needn't ask you out, either. Both of you ought to intuitively know that couplehood means that Saturday evenings are booked. If this is not clear in your relationship, have a conversation about it, and if he squirms, dump him. "Boyfriends" know that weekends were made for Michelob and monogamy.

Instead he should check with *you* if he needs an occasional Saturday night with the boys. And that shouldn't happen too often. Do you want him subject to the bad influence of boys who prefer to be with other boys on date night?

How Does He Handle Disagreement Within the Relationship? Is he shaping up to be a fair fighter or a tyrant?

If you've had no tiny disagreements by month three, then you're not having an honest dating experience. Or you're not seeing each other enough! On the other hand, at this stage you should *not* have had any knockdown, blowout arguments, either. It's much too early and the sweet glow of new love in still blossoming. You should, however, be participating in certain decision making, and your preferences won't always be identical.

The most important questions to ask yourself are: How does he fight? Does he always need to be the winner? Does he needle me with underhanded digs if I win? Is this man willing to hear another side of an issue and adapt if need be? (And am *I?*)

Relationships are all about a seesaw of power. A healthy one goes up and down but finds an equilibrium most of the time. If you're feeling some irritation that your relationship is ruled by his way, his opinions, and his choices, then pay attention to your feelings. This man probably won't change and probably isn't a good boyfriend candidate.

And if he's ever been downright disrespectful, or expressed his anger loudly or physically (even if it's punching a wall), then this man is not emotionally mature enough to have you.

Has He Begun to Reveal Any of His Addictions? We're all addicted to something!

Addictions are part of our culture. Like I said, we're all addicted to something. For me it's caffeine and neurotic analysis of other people's behavior. Most of the time our addictions are innocuous, but if during the "honeymoon" phase of a relationship you start to see steady or inappropriate use of alcohol or drugs, or displays of other addictive behaviors (including sex!), like workaholism or an exercise obsession, this could signal a problem.

Once, after I dated a particularly buffed and brawny boyfriend candidate for about three months, he nonchalantly lit up a joint in front of me. Now, I'm pretty liberal when it comes to marijuana use, though I haven't marched in a "Legalize Hemp" rally. But his use of the drug made me sit up and take notice—he smoked that joint at nine A.M. on his way home from the gym!

This guy couldn't even wait until lunchtime! He couldn't even wait until I was out of his car. His addiction was so ingrained in him that he gave into it at the risk of losing me. I said nothing that morning, thinking it was an aberrant event, so he took my silence as a sign that I condoned the behavior, and after that incident seemed to smoke joints like cigarettes.

Sex addicts are hard to spot. It's hard to tell if a man has a sex addiction in the first few months—you may simply be flattered by all the action. I would be concerned, though, about any man who requires sex more than once a day, or claims to have broken off past relationships because the sex went down to "only" three times a week. Masters and Johnson's famous sex survey said the average for most married couples is five times a month.

As for the workaholic crowd, in the early stage of a relationship he should have no problem telling the white lies needed to get out of a work commitment, if it's for an opportunity to have you in his arms. As an extreme, I once dated a Floridian who used the old "My grandmother died" excuse to come and visit me in Los Angeles. Now, that's bad karma! But when his penis is at the reins, that horse will have no problem coming to water. If he prefers to be at the office, though, and seems to have little time for you, you should prefer to be without him.

QUESTION #6

Is He Sharing His Belongings? It's a basic lesson we learned in kindergarten—share. If he didn't get it then, he doesn't get you now.

Do you get to drive his car if yours is in the shop? Does he mind that you borrowed (and kept) that cozy oversized sweater? Do you wear his bathrobe? These little things seem trite, but they could be an indicator of his ability to share his life.

Plate sharing is an interesting one. It seems to be a dating ritual for a man to feed a woman a bite of his dessert—sort of a way to test your reception to an insertion of a few of his germs into your body. But I know a man (an only child) who goes crazy if a woman so much as mooches a french fry off his plate. Hmmm?

And by the way, you should be willing to share things of yours (but wonder if he prefers your frilly pink bathrobe!). And yet at the same time don't let him become dependent on you for stuff. At this stage he's the resource provider, and the one who should be more than willing to share.

QUESTION #7

What Kind of Relationship Does He Really Have with Mom? This will eventually mirror the relationship he has with you.

I don't mean to harp on the importance of the relationship with our opposite-gender parent, but it really is paramount to one's ability to find and sustain a healthy love relationship.

I once sat at a dinner table with a man and his mom. By dessert I felt as if I were his mistress and she was a subservient wife! He answered her in grunts, complained about the food, stared at the television most of the time, and only paid attention to me during the commercials. And this was supposed to be my *special* Sunday-night dinner to meet his mom!

This is not to say that everyone with bad relationships with their parents will remain single, but it takes work, in the form of some serious soul-searching, to "get over" childhood injustices or tough relationships. The other choice is to have an unconscious relationship where both parties stick their heads in the sand when real issues come up. That's exactly what many people do, but it's not the kind of satisfying relationship a thinking/feeling woman deserves.

There is one perpetually single guy I know who has huge problems letting a woman into his heart. I dated him for about a minute and got out safely early on. However, we did remain friends and I always wondered why he had so much trouble connecting with someone. It wasn't because of any drought— women rained upon his life.

Then one day I called him and was surprised to hear an older woman's voice on the phone. Apparently his mother (whom he'd never spoken about) was visiting from New York. My friend wasn't home, so I explained to her that I was a good friend of her son's and told her that I was calling to thank him for the condolences he sent my way upon the recent deaths of my parents. There was a second of silence and then a mono-toned voice asked, "Does he have your number?"

Now I ask you, if any feeling person hears the phrase "the recent deaths of my parents," what is the natural response? How about "I'm sorry to hear about your loss"? Not this woman. She sounded like an unfeeling computer-mom who simply took down my number. I now have a huge hunch about my friend's "issues" with women.

Has He Begun to Alter His Leisure Activities, Which Were Once So Compatible with Yours? The real *him* is being conveyed to you.

True, we are all on our best behavior during the early stages of dating. We flatter. We accommodate. We facilitate. We conform and we participate, all in the interests of proving to a perspective mate that we are easy to live with and a perfect match for him.

So even if he doesn't enjoy the activity, a courting man will Rollerblade with us, stroll through our favorite art museums, and read the book we're reading just for the shared conversation. Exceptional men will even go shopping with us.

But they can only keep up this charade for so long. And the men you date will be starting to crack after a month or two. I remember the first time a certain boyfriend of mine reached for my remote control while I was cooking dinner. I had been saying to him during the previous (first) month together that I sensed he wasn't being himself when he was in my apartment. I couldn't pinpoint it, but there was a certain uneasiness about him as he hung around my living room flipping through interior design magazines and listening to the soft jazz that I played. Well, the day of the remote-control incident happened late one fall and foreshadowed a frustrating future. He found a Lakers game. Then he found a Cowboys game. Not long after, he found a Rangers game. I didn't know all this programming was even available on my TV! By spring he had moved in with me, and taken my girl-friendly Direct TV satellite package (Lifetime, HBO, & A&E) and expanded it into dozens of sports channels. I think we could even get cricket live from England at two A.M.!

And he watched it all. He began to camp out on the couch from nine to nine on the weekends, and I'm sure any conversation I sent his way probably sounded like a faint, inaudible buzz in the background. He kept promising to spend more time with me after the NBA playoffs, assuring me that there are no sports on TV between the basketball and football seasons. That was until Tiger Woods and the Williams Sisters dominated summer television. Over the course of three year-round sports seasons, I watched my relationship deteriorate and wondered if I shouldn't have paid more attention to that first remote-control episode.

QUESTION #9

Have You Met His Important Friends and Family Members? And has he met yours?

Allowing for the fact that so many people's parents and siblings live thousands of miles away, you should have at least met his accessible inner circle by the three-month mark. This includes his closest friends. And he should have been willing and able to meet yours. This is a big test of a relationship's authenticity.

I was once on the flip side of a well-intended introduction. A man I had been dating in a vacuum (read: I assumed he'd arrived on the planet through the black hole because I had witnessed none of his support group) suggested we take a drive out of town to meet some of his cousins. As the words floated out of his yummy lips, I froze. I was stunned by the epiphany that this simple invitation produced. I suddenly realized that I had no desire to meet anyone who shared his genes. Not that his genes were bad, but the symbolic nature of such an introduction scared the bejesus out of me. I didn't "like" this man enough to be paraded in front of his family. This man, my conscience immediately informed me, was more of a boy-toy than a boyfriend, and I had no business misleading his kinfolk. I declined the invite and our relationship soon soured.

But if the man you *do* desire as a mate is reticent about meeting *your* crowd, then you must wonder if he sees you as authentic girlfriend material. Remember that agoraphobic, music industry executive with the Malibu pad and the lineup of women? Well, he was so afraid to meet my friends that I once had to ambush him by bringing my best friend along unannounced. He wasn't happy about it. And I was alerted to the falseness of our relationship.

Does He Bristle When You Use the B-Word? Go ahead. Take a risk. Just introduce him to someone as your *boyfriend* and see how he reacts.

This was the ultimate litmus test for me. After a consistent three months of dating (with a sexual relationship in full swing), if I have been given no uneasy feelings about his commitment, I would just venture forward and introduce him as my boyfriend to the next person I met.

I have had an array of responses to this. Usually they come later that night when we're both snuggled in bed. I have heard, "Ya know, it kinda freaked me out when you called me your boyfriend today," and "It sounded good to be called your boyfriend today," and "I wondered when you were gonna bring up the boyfriend/girlfriend subject," and "You called me your boyfriend today. Is that what we are?"

Those kinds of responses are all welcome icebreakers to a conversation that men would probably prefer to never have. Most men would undoubtedly prefer to sail through marriage with kids under no title other than "free man."

If his aptitude hasn't exactly shone on the Boyfriend Test and he seems to be sending you all kinds of mixed signals, then watch his body language when you use the B-word. Does he suck in his breath? Does his frame stiffen up just a tad? Does he treat you a little more distantly afterward? He's just given you an answer to the last question of the Boyfriend Test.

Women crave definition. We relish the idea that words can create boundaries, and indeed they can. Bottom line: We want to know where we stand. The truth is, if he's made it through all the other Boyfriend Test questions without hitting any major speed bumps, he is your boyfriend! And you are probably safe in giving your relationship a formal title. Congratulations. Your man has passed the Boyfriend Test.

Ninety-Day Probation
Score Sheet Report Card

Note: This boyfriend candidate starts out with a new rating of 50. From there his behavior either earns or loses him points.

Matt

1 **Do his acquaintances call you by name?**

✓ You've met some of his tertiary world and they regard you only as a stranger. (0)

____ His "people" are quite cordial. (+10)

____ His peripheral people call you by name. (+15)

____ His contacts treat him with a slight air of disdain. (–10)

____ You've met nobody in this part of his world. (-5)

2 **Where does he keep your toothbrush or photo?**

____ He makes sure you leave nothing at his place. (–10)

____ He gives you a drawer or shelf, but your stuff is out of sight. (0)

+10 ✓ You're welcome to leave stuff around. (+10)

____ He displays your photo. (+10)

____ He displays another woman's photo. (–30)

0 -

3 **Does he always reserve Saturday nights for you?**

_____ Yes, always (+15)
_____ Only sometimes (0)
_____ Each week you still have a conversation about it. (–5)
_____ Rarely (–10)
✗ Never (–20)

4 **How does he handle disagreement within the relationship?**

✓ Has an open, fair discussion about it (+20)
_____ Shuts down and gets silent (0)
_____ Walks out (–5)
_____ Snaps at you (–15)
_____ Sends nasty little digs at you (sarcastic, condescending, mocking) (–20)
_____ Raises the volume of his voice (–30)

+20

5 **Has he begun to reveal any of his addictions?**

_____ Cigarettes (–5)
_____ Alcohol (–20)
_____ Caffeine (–5)
_____ Any other drugs (–30)
_____ Exercise (–5)
_____ Work (–5)
0 Sex (–30)

6 Is he sharing his belongings?

_____ Lends stuff but really keeps track of your usage and states his return policy (–10)

_____ Very generous with his personal stuff, almost without boundaries (0)

_____ Will buy you stuff, but won't lend his own (+10)

_____ Some things he'll part with, others not (+15)

_____ No, none at all (–20)

7 What kind of relationship does he really have with Mom?

_____ Too close (–10)

_✓__ Too distant (–10)

_____ Seems to have loving contact and no big issues with her (+10)

8 Has he begun to alter his leisure activities, which were once so compatible with yours?

_✓__ Yes, and you have no problems with the "real" him. (0)

_____ Yes, and there's one or two activities that you'd prefer he still do with you. (–5)

_____ You discuss your wish for more common interests and he doesn't alter his behavior. (–10)

_____ You discuss your wish for more common interests and he makes a better effort. (+15)

_____ You suddenly wonder if you have anything in common besides eating and sex. (–15)

9 **Have you met his important friends and family members?**

_____ No family because they live too far away (0)

_____ Have met his closest friends (+10)

✓ Have met some family, some friends (+10)

_____ Have met few truly close people, only peripheral people (−10) +10

_____ Have met no one in his life (−20)

10 **Does he bristle when you use the B-word?**

_____ He sucks in his breath. (−5)

_____ He stiffens up. (−5)

_____ He walks away. (−10)

_____ He faints. (−15)

_____ He gets defensive. (−20) − 10

✓ He ignores it. (−10)

_____ He starts to use the "G-word (not _golf_, the other G-word!). (+15)

_____ It sparks a healthy conversation about commitment. (+20)

GRADING THE NINETY-DAY TEST

Note: Get out your notebooks and pencils, gals: This grade is calculated by adding the scores of *all five parts* of the Boyfriend Test and then dividing by five.

The candidate must score an A+ grade to be worthy of the moniker of boyfriend.

- ■ **Exceptional (90–100) A+**

- ■ **Excellent (80–89) A**

- ■ **Very Good (75–79) B+**

- ■ **Good (70–74) B**

- ■ **Satisfactory (65–69) C+**

- ■ **Minimum Pass (60–64) C**

- ■ **Failure (50–59) D**

- ■ **Complete Failure (0–49) F**

a couple's
REPORT
CARD

So now you have a bona fide boyfriend. What, besides the obvious, do you do with him? Well, you just keep becoming a better girlfriend. You keep reminding him (and yourself) of your boundaries and you try your darndest not to get trapped in traditional gender roles that tend to be unfair to women. That sounds easy, but it's a lot of conscious work.

I'd like to help you out a bit by explaining my definition of a successful relationship and finally, by sharing a personal story of my own search for a good boyfriend—the journey that gave me the insight to write this book.

relation-
ship clues

> A love affair is a delicate
> balancing act between a person's
> needs and wants, producing a
> tension that has raged since the
> days of our earliest ancestors.
> —William Allman, *The Stone Age Present*

This book, while helping you find and keep
the right man, offers little guidance on
how to actually *have* a relationship. The
union of strangers who become family is
about as hard to define as the black hole. The pairing of two
unique hearts becomes something separate from the two individuals and is unlike that of any other couple.

William Allman, in *The Stone Age Present,* explains couplehood well. "At its heart, human sexuality has always been a
dialogue of compromise between men and women, a coopera-

tive bargain where neither partner gets everything they wish, yet both ultimately reap far more satisfaction than they could have had alone."

Having told you that, I'd rather not leave you creeping down the tunnel of a relationship without a flashlight. For all my blunders and lessons, I have learned a few things that may help you in the harrowing halls of long-term monogamy. What follows is a brief definition of a healthy relationship, along with some down-the-road "heads-up."

Every relationship has rules, whether unspoken or not (since I run on estrogen, I prefer the spoken kind), and all relationships have curious practices that, when observed by an outsider, can seem very strange. I know couples who take separate vacations, who share the finances in "unfair" proportions, who split housework like it's the eighteenth century, and who have wild arguments just so they can have passionate lovemaking afterward. All of these practices don't suit me but seem to suit those couples just fine. They are all functioning couples.

So what defines a functioning couple? In layperson's terms, a functioning couple helps create a safe and respectful environment for both partners to air their feelings. It allows both members a voice.

It also allows for the kind of friction that helps us to grow instead of beating us down. A functioning couple is not in agreement all the time. Each dispute will end with one winner and one loser. But those roles flip-flop a lot. And each time a disagreement arises, a functioning couple grows closer, wiser, and more aware of each other's boundaries.

Oh, and there's one other crucial part of the definition: The woman is usually (though not always) the conduit for closeness. In a relationship between a man and a woman, the woman usually holds the cards of emotional intimacy. For all kinds of reasons—some anthropological, some cultural, but all frustrating—men in our world today have trouble expressing themselves and empathizing with the feelings of others. Whether it's because, as ancient hunters, if they stopped to enjoy a sunset, they might have gotten eaten by a lion, or because their mothers told them that big boys don't cry, our men need some coaxing and some patience from us when it comes to emotions.

They also have trouble listening to us vent without trying to fix something. You complain about your boss's tyranny, and your man tells you to get a new job. Period. But you say you aren't *that* unhappy about your work environment, you just needed to express your anxiety. Most men, however, still think you're asking them for a solution. A great man understands that women work differently. The majority of men don't.

What Is a "Functioning" Relationship?

So, if a functional relationship is one where we hold the keys to both his and her emotional lockers, and we as women often do most of the housework and child rearing, then where does the "functional" part come in? This definition of a relationship can make it

sound like it functions well for *him,* but not necessarily
for *her.*

Well, a functioning couple may not split the bills, the
housework, the social duties, or the child care equally. But if
all these things are averaged out, there should be an overall
feeling of fairness. The actual division of labor—whether physical, emotional, or financial—may not always look to outsiders
as fair, but the relationship still supports, protects, and stimu-
lates both partners.

The "functioning" comes from shared projects (like children, a home renovation project, a shared hobby, or a business venture) where both partners take satisfaction from their
contributions. The functioning comes when a woman learns to
read a man who may talk in grunts. The functioning comes
when anger is expressed as a thought, not an action. The
functioning comes when a man notices a woman feeling down
and doesn't try to cheer her up, but just stays near and listens. The functioning comes when a couple exchanges glances
at a dinner party and both immediately know the funny story
that will be exchanged between them later. The functioning
comes when an impasse has been reached and somehow the
couple finds themselves laughing about it. The functioning
comes when one partner grows and the other wiggles and
squirms to find a new comfort zone while accommodating the
changed relationship.

Some relationships transcend the definition of "functioning" and extend to something even more special and fulfilling.
In her book *Love Between Equals,* sociologist Pepper Schwartz
interviewed what she calls "peer couples" (couples who

equally share everything—money, household chores, and child rearing) to develop a profile of these exceptional unions. "More often than not," she writes, "the women in these relationships were good communicators and were clear about how they wanted and needed to be treated; they had a strong sense of what was a fair deal. The men had the ability to understand and support their partner's wishes. Most of these couples had to negotiate early in the relationship—and keep negotiating throughout it—to keep it a partnership, rather than watching it slip into more traditional (gender based) roles."

It Takes Time to Create a Relationship

In this book, you've been able to determine in ninety days if a man is deserving of the moniker of "boyfriend." (It's not my goal to educate you on how to have a great relationship—tons of other books do that.) But I will say that once he becomes your significant other, it takes a great deal of time before a long-term trusting bond is established. It make take even longer to merge your lives into one.

We all know couples who had a whirlwind romance and landed under one roof, married or not, within months. Some of them have lucked out and created a functioning union, but they are the minority. I have been in many a whirlwind myself, and the outcome usually resembled a scene from *Twister*.

It puts an unfair pressure on a relationship to move in together, get married, or have children, before spending the critical duration needed to create emotional intimacy. I know this because I have met all three of these challenges with various men in my life. Although I'll never regret conceiving my angel daughter, I am sad that her parents were still learning relationship lessons during her infancy.

At a minimum, a relationship takes one year to ferment. The first year of dating is burdened by the newlywed syndrome: It's new. You're both polite. You behave like houseguests in fluffy white bathrobes.

It is when we pass through the seasons for the second time that we start to create traditions, fall into familiar and comfortable routines, and begin to build memories together— "Remember last Christmas when we...?" In the second year, we become ourselves. We should be saying *ouch* when one of our precious boundaries is stepped on. That bathrobe is starting to look worn. It fits your body better with the few snags and stains.

By year three the pockets of that bathrobe are filled with snotty Kleenex, a stray hairpin, and some melting M&Ms. And he doesn't notice.

I'll Be Your Mother If You'll Be Mine

The search for a partner is, in some sense, also a search for the parents we left behind. In many ways our man functions as our mother and our father. And we do the same for him. Aspects of this "playacting" are unavoidable. It's how our brain was imprinted. The difficulty comes from the fact that we may have had flawed parenting that we are now trying to replicate.

Our parents made mistakes because their parents made worse ones. No one is to blame. It is evolution. We'll be better than our parents were, and our kids will do an even better job with our grandchildren. (At least we hope it will go that way.)

But what if our parenting was so awful that we have no idea how to create love or intimacy? What if we were imprinted with abuse, abandonment, and longing?

In her provocative book, *The Continuum Concept,* Jean Liedloff makes a case for the benefits of a twelve-month "infant in arms" phase, pointedly reminding mothers that our ancient people did not own strollers, car seats, and cribs, and that our human psychological development is dependent on a very slow separation from womb to dorm room. Liedloff's theory is that if a tiny baby's first impression of the world is one of warmth, comfort, and security, then he or she will grow up to re-create that as an adult. But she has a tragic prediction for those who miss this loving attention:

> For people with extensive requirements—people whose early lives have left them without enough fulfillment even to compensate satisfactorily with another person and his needs—the search for a mate is often a sad and endless one. They have been betrayed in infancy and their longings are wide and deep. The fear of being betrayed again can be so strong that the moment there is danger of finding a companion, they flee in terror to

avoid putting the candidate to the test and being reminded, unbearably, that they are not lovable in the unconditional way they require.

Any of the men you meet may have had such awful experiences. Or your own infancy may have been bad. If you have read this book and felt empathy for the heartbreak you've heard about in these pages, then you may be a woman of weak boundaries. If you often fail to speak up when someone affronts your soul because you don't want to hurt their feelings, then you may "people-please" to your own detriment. If you find yourself running from nice guys and discover way too many bad boys in your bed, then you are definitely hurting yourself.

Your pain could have many different causes, but I agree with Jean Liedloff that the psyche is created in the first twelve months of life. At the same time we are growing at such a rapid pace, we are also trying to make sense of the world, to trust it or not. First impressions can be lasting. Follow an unhappy infancy with a childhood of hurts, and you'll understand why so many of us have had trouble creating a lasting bond.

I cannot tell you what life lessons brought you to the place you are in your life; I may be empathetic, but I am not telepathic. I can, however, be brave and share my own story, complete with feelings, outcomes, and mendings, in the hopes that some of it may ring true for you.

my story: bad boys and bad poetry

> Courtship is often a testing ground to determine how far each partner's infantile needs will be met
>
> —Jean Liedloff, *The Continuum Concept*

I've had a hard time with men. And I'm quite sure that if you asked many of the men I've dated, they'd say that I wasn't exactly a picnic, either. As you've gleaned from the abundant anecdotes in this book, I spent many years dating inappropriate men. And I learned a lot about myself in the process.

My pattern was this: Most of the time I sought tall, deep-voiced men who acted indifferent to me—at least after I'd had sex with them. Before that they were usually well skilled at courting rituals. And I lapped up that wine-and-dinner routine. I was so attracted to the idea of feeling loved, even if it were an illusion. But once I gave my heart, my boyfriends would either take off or take the panties off of another woman, and I'd take my abandonment issues to the next man who'd fulfill my fears. I wrote bad poetry in my diary along my broken-hearted journey that reveals anger, pain, and confusion. I'm willing to share some of this bad poetry with you because maybe you can relate *and* laugh!

> My innocence
> you took like a thief
> when it was left unlocked
> you hawked
> and jocked
> and mocked
> You got me in bed
> Now I put you to bed
> Your rough exterior
> And hollow interior
> pushed from my thoughts
> Thanks for what you've taught!

I called these men "Advance Retreaters." They always advanced hard and strong in pursuit of love and then retreated when I turned to offer love in return. They would take longer and longer to return my calls. They would screen their voice mail rather than pick up the phone. They were less and less available. I really felt sheer agony around these guys, along with deep feelings of loss. But I still unconsciously continued to repeat the pattern of choosing this kind of man because it felt somehow familiar to me. Upon closer inspection, my silly poems now give me clues about previously hidden issues:

> I'm not afraid to see you go
> You're cutest from behind
> But one thing I do surely know
> if you stay I'll lose my mind

When my "Advance Retreaters" were in retreat mode, I medicated myself with another kind of man. He was the "Sweet Thing"—pretty compliant, although emotionally out of touch with himself, more than a little insecure, and someone who tended to take any kind of licking I doled out. He often made less money than me, or was less attractive, or worked in a less glamorous business than television (not possible, I say), and he was delighted to satisfy his insecurities by being with me. Remember, at the time, I marketed myself as a bleached blonde with a smart mouth.

> At the club I felt his fit, dark physique
> sliding past me again.
> This time I didn't let him escape a
> conversation with me.
> He was so sweet. Shy. Said he was
> twenty-nine.
> Looked twenty-three.
> Works at his father's restaurant.
> Simple. No flash. A breath of fresh air.
> I gave him my number.

But then, when the emphatic connection that I craved didn't materialize with one of my "Sweet Things," I usually had another affair with an "Advance Retreater," whose advances were so darned exciting and whose retreats were so anger-invoking.

Back and forth I rebounded, from men who were amenable but immature to men who were even more immature but whom I thought were stoic gods or irresistible Dream Men. And all along I thought I was doing the right thing by being kind, accommodating, and spending way too much time attempting to save *them* from *their* emotional misery. Boy, was I in denial.

My Wake-Up Call

I've told you about one of the greatest life-changing events I've experienced. My parents, in a relatively short period of time, both succumbed to cancer, my mother to breast cancer, followed by my father to lung cancer. I was thirty-two and still clueless about why my love life was going so badly. Of the many things I mourned upon their passing was the fact that, even if I could get it together to have a healthy relationship, my children would never know their grandparents.

As a temporary salve, the week after I buried my father, I stupidly boarded a plane to New Zealand to hook up with my latest "Advance Retreater." Only he hadn't revealed himself as a Houdini yet. (Maybe he didn't have to hint at any retreating tendencies—he lived seven thousand miles away!)

Together we celebrated my birthday with a romantic dinner at a five-star resort, and after some delicious lovemaking, he murmured to me in a throaty baritone that he thought he was falling in love. At that moment I though I'd achieved nirvana—an "Advance Retreater" who uttered the L-word! Within weeks, this man wasn't taking my phone calls. Here's the poem I wrote about this loser:

> Yes, he was my overdose
> that made me look real close
> and see the beefcake was beef jerky.
> It was time to go cold turkey.

So with an "Advance Retreater" running from me and the deaths of my parents to mourn, I was in acute pain, though on the outside you couldn't see that. I was a reporter and host on the national magazine show *Extra.* I was developing my own television production company. I was helping to run a charity. I was chairing a women's investment group, and I was buying and remodeling my first home. That's when I wasn't at the gym or having a facial.

This hectic schedule was just a mask, a way to keep busy, to hold back my tears. When I was alone, there was another me. Los Angeles is a car culture and solitude often appears on freeways, behind the privacy of tinted windows and Armani shades, and every time I got behind the wheel of my car, I couldn't stop the rush of tears. Then, most nights alone in my room, I'd listen to Tracy Chapman or James Taylor and bawl like a baby. Despite my wonderfully supportive girlfriends, I can't ever remember feeling so alone.

Ironically, during much of that time I blamed my crying jags on PMS, so I sought all the herbal remedies for PMS that I could. From melatonin to evening primrose oil to St. John's wort, if there was a natural substance that promised to relieve the psychological symptoms of PMS, I tried it. Nowadays I know better. I was in emotional crisis. (And besides, even if it were PMS, I believe that's when women have their most powerful moments of clarity!)

Because nothing was working to alleviate things, I tried a shrink. With a referral from a friend, I found myself in a full-fledged psychiatrist's office—I was so skeptical about the science of psychotherapy, I needed a medical school graduate with a title of "Dr." As it turned out, she was warm and loving and unlike any M.D. I'd ever known. She taught me to meditate and suggested I try celibacy for a while, just to clear my head. It was a scary jump. For me, giving up men was like giving up a drug. But I had to, in order to reveal my underlying issues.

Within a few months of not dating, I was feeling much better and stopped going to see her. I raved about the amazing results I had gotten from therapy in such a short period of time. I felt healed. I told all my friends they should try it, too.

I started a new life with long walks on the beach, daily meditations, plenty of books, and no men. It was bliss. In truth, though, I was in another kind of denial, as exhibited in this snippet of "verse":

> Should the quiet drown out the noise
> you'll hear your inner voice

you know it's whispering to you
and you don't know what to do

Hit by a Truck

arianne Willamson tells a great story about
celibacy in one of her inspirational lectures
to women. She says she thought she was
healing by being celibate, but in truth she
was only avoiding. When she left celibacy behind, she said it
felt like walking out of her house and getting hit by a truck.

Mine was a Mack truck. After one year, I stepped out of
the house (i.e., celibacy) and onto the street—and got myself
pregnant.

Of course, with hindsight, I see that the entrance of a tiny
angel into my life was the greatest gift I could ever have imag-
ined. There is a saying, "Although grown-ups produce children, it is children who produce adults." The peace, wisdom,
and confidence that were ushered into my life by motherhood
go unmatched by any other life-altering event. But it didn't
come without a struggle.

After a year out of "the life," I met a man who gave me
two of the greatest gifts (and challenges) ever: an embryo and
a relatively stable relationship. Here was a man who wouldn't
run away from me like an "Advance Retreater," but who also
wouldn't behave as compliantly as my "Sweet Things." There
was turmoil in our relationship for some time as I adjusted to
this new kind of man and he adjusted to domestic life after
years as a loner.

This was also an opportunity to get in touch with my deepest feelings. When I became pregnant, the hormonal changes in my body, coupled with the triggers to uterine and infantile memories that pregnancy can elicit, brought a major emotional awakening. In short, being pregnant helped me finally get to the bottom of some of my issues with men—although I don't recommend this treatment!

Back to the Shrink

In my second trimester I sought professional guidance again. This new therapist had a different style. No prescriptions to meditate. No mandates to be celibate. No homework. Just quiet, nonjudging nods that gave me space to hear myself think.

In her gentle manner, she chaperoned me back to my childhood. Time and time again, she asked me to analyze my feelings about men (and everything else) and draw bridges to my childhood—to find early occurrences of the same kind of feelings. So I did.

I used to think I had a *Leave It to Beaver* childhood. My parents stayed together. We were middle class. My father was an officer in the navy. My mother was a homemaker. I had two brothers who were very close in age to me. We lived in the suburbs. We took many family vacations. On the surface, it all looked healthy.

But as I've said, regardless of seemingly ideal surroundings, the process of growing up is painful in itself. As toddlers, we are mentally ready for tasks like climbing stairs before our bodies can do it safely, and later in adolescence and teenaged life, there are all kinds of occasions when we are physically ready for something but not yet psychologically prepared. And during all those frustrating times, if we are not allowed to express our feelings of anger, or fear, or whatever, we start to mistrust ourselves, to deny our own feelings. That's where weak boundaries begin—an inability to hear one's inner voice because it has been disciplined out of us.

In my case, I discovered there were other, less common, childhood challenges. With the help of that sensitive psychologist, I stripped away the storybook aspects of my childhood and dared to feel childish emotions again. A father in the navy isn't a father at home. Weeks or months of an absentee father can create huge abandonment issues in young girls. I lived my childhood between ship dockings in a kind of panic, waiting for my protector to return. "Protector?" you may ask. "Protection from whom or from what?"

That answer came easily once my toddler life was examined in detail. Like some of you who are reading this book, I was born as part of the baby boom that shaped our culture after World War II. I was sandwiched between two boys. My older brother was eleven months older than me and my "little" brother was a year and a half younger. Yes, my mother had three children under the age of four with no household help! And being that we were always living on some new military base, she often had no family support of any kind. My mother was overwhelmed and our home was chaos much of the time.

My older brother, bless his tiny heart, was an angry child, angry that his time of nurturing had been cut short by the arrival of another infant—me. He was a brilliant, wild child who tormented me no end. Mental pictures of my early child-hood show me at the bottom of toddler skirmishes, screaming for help. I was caught between the physicality of two rowdy boys. Yes, I felt unprotected.

Aha! Could this yearning for Daddy to come home and save me relate to my penchant for enormous men with deep voices? Could my "Advance Retreaters" be my protective father, who arrived for loving though brief stays, only to aban-don me again? I think there is perhaps a connection.

I suspect that there is a tiny girl inside of me who saw these large men with deep voices as a kind of father figure who were to protect me from the "little men with high voices" (my brothers) who tormented me. So who might the "little men with high voices" be represented by in my adult life? Well, as I see it, those are my peers. They are men my own age, size, and income level, whom I've had such a hard time making emotional connections with. Back in 1992, before my parents became ill and before my emotional wake-up call, I wrote this in my diary:

> I wish to make peace with my peers
> to overcome all of my fears
> of naughty boys
> scoring higher in math
> excelling in sports
> and having the last laugh
> I wish for my mind to clear
> those memories of painful jeers.
> I wish to make peace with my peers
> to be able to call one of them dear

to be counted as equal
not the latest sequel

But my issues ran even deeper. As I progressed in my own therapy and became a mother myself, I learned about the deep attachments that an infant must feel for a caregiver, most often a mother. That close bond becomes the infrastructure of tools of emotional intimacy. If a helpless infant doesn't "attach" to someone, and be assured that their every need will be met, they can grow up to distrust all relationships. If a mother takes too long to appear and comfort a crying infant, the result can be a grown human who feels abandoned easily, or seeks relationships that don't meet their basic needs, because *that* feels normal to them.

But how could the required amount of "attachment" have been accomplished with me? How could my mother, a victim of a baby-factory era, have given each of us the individual nurturing that humans require—access to milk-filled breasts, holding, rocking, consoling? No, I am quite sure that if three babies cried at once, two were left to panic alone, at least until she calmed one. Talk about early abandonment training.

Enter my "Sweet Things." These kind, compliant men were probably some compensation for the maternal nurturing that I missed out on. In a strange way, I believe these men were my mother figures, far from peers, yet loving and accommodating. By the way, I also tended to unconsciously select *women* friends who, in many ways, fulfilled this role. They were kind, "people-pleasing" girlfriends, and I was blessed to have them on the rocky road I walked with men.

Our Parents Aren't to Blame

When we embark on a journey toward personal growth and recall the pain associated with childhood experiences, there may be a tendency to blame our parents. I remind you again that our parents are not at fault. They did the best job they could, given the resources available to them and the emotional skills they possessed. As I've said, they were probably better parents than their own parents, and your grandparents were probably better parents than their parents. So how far back do we go to place blame? Cavemen?

Evolution means that each generation has more knowledge and more insight than the previous one and works harder to propagate the species. In recent generations that knowledge has been directed toward the emotional development of babies.

All this is not to say that we shouldn't feel angry about how we may have been parented. Anger is a healthy emotion and one that should be felt in order to heal. But when we analyze our past, we should judge not what was done to us, but rather how we reacted to what was done to us.

My parents, bless their souls, did an amazing job rearing three narrowly spaced siblings to reproductive age. Our hunter/gatherer ancestors would not have had such odds for offspring survival.

Growing Up Is Growing In

In the last few years of therapy I have learned to create an observing eye that helps me analyze my past, decipher my present, and attempt to influence my future. In analyzing my past I came up with the Boyfriend Test. I saw with clarity my self-damaging decisions about men and my need for some clear guidelines to spot unhealthy relationships before they occurred. Although I had made bad choices, I now know it was not my fault. I now understand why I did what I did. Over time, I have become very clear about my boundaries. I fell in love. We are now about to head into our fifth year together, and we have a beautiful daughter. And I wanted a way to share my newfound knowledge with others through humor and real-life dating stories that might ring true for other women. I hope this book has accomplished that.

bibliography

Allman, William F. *The Stone Age Present,* pp. 110, 112–13, 118. New York: Simon & Schuster, 1994.

Bach, Richard. *Illusions: The Adventures of a Reluctant Messiah.* New York: Dell Publishing, 1977.

Blum, Deborah. *Sex on the Brain: The Biological Differences Between Men and Women.* New York: Penguin Books, 1997.

Buss, David M. *The Evolution of Desire: Strategies of Human Mating.* New York: Basic Books, 1994.

Carter, Steven, and Julia Sokol. *Men Who Can't Love (And What a Smart Woman Can Do About It).* New York: MJF Books, 1987.

Chopra, Deepak. *The Seven Spiritual Laws of Success: A Practical Guide to the Fulfillment of Your Dreams.* San Rafael, Calif.: Amber-Allen Publishing, 1994.

Daly, Martin, and Margo Wilson. *Sex, Evolution and Behavior* (second edition), p. 72. Belmont, Calif.: Wadsworth Publishing Company, 1978.

Douglas, Nik. *Spiritual Sex.* New York: Pocket Books, 1997.

Fielding, Helen. *Bridget Jones's Diary,* p. 38. New York: Penguin Putnam, 1996.

Frager, Robert, and James Fadiman. *Personality and Personal Growth* (fourth edition). Longman, 1998.

Gerber, Magda. *Dear Parents: Caring for Infants with Respect.* Los Angeles: RIE, 1998.

Goleman, Daniel. *Emotional Intelligence: Why It Can Matter More Than IQ.* New York: Bantam Books, 1995.

Hoffman, Alice. *Local Girls,* p. 103. New York: Penguin Putnam, 1999.

Hollander, Dory, Ph.D. *101 Lies Men Tell Women and Why Women Believe Them.* New York: HarperCollins, 1995.

Hrdy, Sarah Blaffer, Ph.D. *Mother Nature: A History of Mothers, Infants, and Natural Selection.* New York: Pantheon Books, 1999.

Ledoux, Joseph. *The Emotional Brain: The Mysterious Underpinnings of Emotional Life.* New York: Simon & Schuster, 1996.

Leidloff, Jean. *The Continuum Concept,* p. 112. New York: Perseus Press, 1986 (A Merloyd Lawrence Book).

Lerner, Harriet Goldhor, Ph.D. *The Dance of Anger.* New York: Harper & Row, 1985.

Miller, Alice. *The Drama of the Gifted Child: The Search for the True Self.* New York: Basic Books, 1996.

Peck, M. Scott, M.D. *The Road Less Traveled: A New Psychology of Love, Traditional Values, and Spiritual Growth.* New York: Touchstone, 1978.

————. *Further Along the Road Less Traveled: The Unending Journey Toward Spiritual Growth*. New York: Touchstone, 1993.

————. *The Road Less Traveled and Beyond: Spiritual Growth in an Age of Anxiety*. New York: Simon & Schuster, 1997.

Sapolsky, Robert M. *The Trouble with Testosterone, and Other Essays on the Biology of the Human Predicament*. New York: Scribner, 1997.

Schwartz, Pepper, Ph.D. *Love Between Equals: How Peer Marriage Really Works*. New York: The Free Press, 1994.

Small, Meredith F. *Female Choices: Sexual Behavior of Female Primates*. Cornell, N.Y.: Cornell University Press, 1993.

Stringer, Christopher, and Robin McKie. *African Exodus: The Origins of Modern Humanity*. New York: Henry Holt and Company, 1996.

Tesina, Tina, Ph.D., and Elizabeth Friar Williams. *The Ten Smartest Decisions a Woman Can Make Before Forty*. Deerfield Beach, Fla.: Health Communications, 1998.

Vaughan, Susan C., M.D. *The Talking Cure,* p. 185. New York: Grosset/Putnam, 1997.

Viorst, Judith. *Imperfect Control: Our Lifelong Struggles with Power and Surrender*. New York: Simon & Schuster, 1998.

Williamson, Marianne. *A Woman's Worth*. New York: Random House, 1993.

Yalom, Irwin, Ph.D. *Love's Executioner*. New York: HarperCollins, 1990.

about the author

Wendy Walsh is a journalist with a knack for taking science and personal experience and turning it into practical and sometimes funny advice. Drawing from the work of anthropologists, psychologists, and biologists, Walsh's book is sisterly comfort in the trenches of the love wars.

Walsh is a former Los Angeles news anchor and entertainment correspondent for the *Weekend Today Show*. Her style and personality have landed her hosting positions on many nationally syndicated television shows, including *Extra, How'd They Do That?*, CNet's *TV.Com, Starz Movie News, Motor Trend Television,* as well as specials for NBC, ABC, HBO, CNBC, and Fox Sports.

Her personal life has been riddled with boyfriend candidates. Some she hired. Many she fired. And along the way she learned to interview well. Says Walsh, "I wish I could have a pair of Kenneth Coles for every time I fell in love with someone's potential. I eventually learned that potential can't love you back."

for more
information

If you would like to learn more about Wendy Walsh and
The Boyfriend Test, please visit www.theboyfriendtest.com.